Best Stories from New Writers

Best Stories from New Writers

Edited by Linda S. Sanders

 Writer's Digest Books Cincinnati, Ohio

Best Stories from New Writers.
Copyright 1989 by Writers Digest Books.
Printed and bound in the United States of America.
All rights reserved. No part of this book may be
reproduced in any form or by electronic or
mechanical means including information storage
and retrieval systems without permission in writing
from the publisher, except in a review.
Published by Writer's Digest Books, an imprint of
F & W Publications, Inc.
1507 Dana Avenue,
Cincinnati, Ohio 45207.

First Edition.

92 91 90 89 88   5 4 3 2 1

Library of Congress Cataloging-in-Publication Data

Best stories from new writers / edited by Linda Sanders.
    p. cm.
  ISBN 0–89879–367–X
    1. Short stories, American. 2. American fiction—20th century.
I. Sanders, Linda (Linda S.)
PS648.S5B47   1989
813'.0108054—dc20   89–14716
                                                  CIP

$\mathcal{C}$ONTENTS

When I began *Best Stories from New Writers* nearly a year ago, I didn't know what to expect. The idea was to publish ten to fifteen of the best stories we could find by writers who had never been published before. Putting those stories into an anthology would, we thought, bring added recognition to strong new writers, help expand the market for good writing, and encourage and instruct other writers still struggling to break into print.

But nothing like this had been done before. Would we find enough stories of quality by new writers? Would editors nominate their best stories, help me track down the authors, explain why they chose the stories they did? Would authors still trying to establish themselves be willing to talk about the mistakes they made, as well as what they did right?

So I began this project with high hopes, tempered by doubts. But on every front, my highest expectations were met and exceeded. Hard-working, underpaid (and sometimes *un*paid) editors responded with enthusiasm and gave willingly of their time and thoughtfulness—in return for nothing more than further recognition for the authors they discovered. Writers, even those who have received a good deal of attention since these stories were first published, were delighted and honored. (And unassuming. One was so dubious that his story had been chosen for a serious collection that he asked whether he'd have to *pay* anything to be included.)

And the stories! So many of them were heart-felt and honest, moving in the way fiction ought to be. They weren't as practiced as the fiction of more established writers, and many times they were better for it. They spoke to me of so many human things: death, separation, frustration, families dissolving, cultures changing, illness, vanity, war, fear, and dreams. They were wonderful.

So *Best Stories from New Writers* is everything I'd hoped it would be. It is, first, a collection of fine fiction. These twelve stories are richly textured, exploring the depth and significance of everyday experience. The characters who populate these stories are—like all of us—doing the best they can as they move through life. Sometimes what they do seems simple on the surface—standing up to a boss in "Among the Righteous" or speaking up for someone who's misunderstood in "Little Saigon." Sometimes they must do nothing, as in "Do Not Disturb" or the wonderfully understated "Sunday." And at other times they are called on to do the heroic—surviving the horrors of Vietnam in "The Village" or protecting a brother who is a local hero in "Cecil Grounded."

But no matter what, the people we meet in these stories carry on. No matter what they face—from the desolation of the South Bronx to the painful disruption of a family—they are not defeated by it. Only one loses the battle, but at the very last moment, he recognizes his enemy for what it is and so, too, overcomes.

That, to me, is the common thread of these stories. The amazing, resilient strength of the human spirit. The courage and determination and, well, the *goodness* of people.

But this collection is more than a good read. It offers special insight into how writers and editors work. Twenty-four people— the author of each story and the editor who chose it—gave me glimpses into their creative processes. The writers told me, as best they could, where the ideas came from and how they developed. They told me about getting rejected and dejected. They told of rewriting and of refusing to rewrite. And they spoke of wonderful moments when the writing came easily and surely, times when their fingers couldn't move fast enough to keep up with the words.

The editors told me of the thrill of finding a new writer, of suggestions made and accepted, of characters who compelled them and voices that excited them. They had much more to say about what was good in the writing found here than about what was bad, and all of them, to the very last one, urged all struggling writers to keep at it.

Taken together, these stories and interviews have something very special to say. The message is a hopeful one, and anyone who loves fiction—whether as writer or reader—should take heart. I certainly did.

Since this is the first *Best Stories,* perhaps I should explain how it was put together. I had imagined the process to be a fairly straightforward one—I'd set the rules and then follow them. It didn't turn out that way.

I began by asking seventy-five fiction editors at magazines across the country to nominate stories they felt should be included. I wrote to all kinds of magazines—literary, commercial, mainstream, science fiction, mystery, well-known, and little known—since the idea was to find the best new writers no matter where they'd been published. Each editor could nominate as many stories as he or she wanted (one magazine nominated nine).

To be eligible, the story had to be the author's first professionally published work of fiction and to have appeared between June 1, 1986 and May 30, 1988.

It sounds simple, doesn't it? It wasn't.

The trouble began with the phrase "professionally published." I knew that term was a bit vague when I used it, but I could find no clear-cut way to draw the line. I didn't want to rule someone out because they'd published a story in their college newspaper or their writing group's newsletter. But many of the best—most professional—literary magazines don't pay writers and don't have large circulations. I couldn't use those criteria to establish what a professional publication was.

In the end, I never found a way to define it. I tried to include as many authors as possible, but ruled out anyone whose prior publication was in a magazine I thought was serious. Subjective, I know, but the only way I could find.

The trickiest call was this one: After E. S. Goldman's "Way to the Dump" was chosen, he told me that forty-five years ago he had one story published pseudonymously in *Adventure,* a pulp that folded years ago. He was in the Navy then and had no thoughts of becoming a serious writer. I decided not to disqualify him. That first story was so long ago and so minor, accepting "Way to the Dump" didn't seem to violate the spirit of what we were trying to accomplish.

I also decided first publication meant just that—not the first story *sold,* but the first to actually appear in print.

To make the selections I worked with Howard I. Wells III of Wells & Associates, editor and consultant. Both of us were readers long before we were editors, and it was as readers that we approached the task.

We read the stories without knowing where they'd been published, so we wouldn't be influenced by any particular magazine's reputation, and each of us came up with our own entirely subjective rating system. We didn't try to establish any kind of criteria or formula for judging the stories, since the only true standard for good fiction is that it move you.

I believe the process worked, that these truly are the twelve best stories from new writers. There were other stories I longed to print, because they held promise or because they were fresh or because I liked what the author was trying to do. (There were also some stories I didn't like at all. Stories that would make other writers think, "Well, if *this* got published, *I* can surely get published too." Maybe it would have been more encouraging to have reprinted those.)

But we couldn't print everything we liked, and so we chose the twelve we liked most. I had hoped that the final selection would include stories from other genres—because those stories seem to be overlooked by most anthologies—but it didn't work out that way. Perhaps that's because the percentage of nominations from genres other than mainstream was small.

I'd also anticipated that we'd include more quirky or innovative stories. But most new writers (at least those getting published) seem to be working in the traditional narrative form. The cases where something dramatically different is called for are rare. We didn't find any.

Introduction

. . . .

5

When the final decisions had been made, I found myself facing another tough call. My letter to the fiction editors had promised that the stories would be printed exactly as they had first appeared. I didn't want to edit the stories, as is done in many collections, because that sometimes damages the stories and because it would defeat the point—how can readers see what's getting published and learn from that if the stories have been changed substantially?

But when I talked to the authors, several of them wanted changes to their stories. They had discovered glitches that got through the editing process. In one case, some numbers didn't add up; in another, a particular word didn't seem right; in a third, a technical detail was wrong. Nothing too major.

Until Amy Lippman. *Mademoiselle* fiction editor Eileen Schnurr asked Lippman to make a few changes to her story, and Lippman reluctantly agreed. She didn't like the changes, though, and wanted the story to appear without them here. The most important difference was she wanted me to restore two sentences that had been cut from the end.

That was no minor change.

I decided, once again, to go with my gut feelings. I could understand why an author wouldn't want her work to appear in a form she didn't like a second time. But I wanted anyone who read this collection to get a real understanding of what first-published stories were like.

So I let the authors make any minor changes they wanted on the condition that they'd discuss those changes with me in the interviews. That way the writers would be happy and readers could learn some interesting inside stuff. (A full discussion of Lippman's ending follows her story.)

I don't know if I succeeded in bending the rules in a way that was fair to everyone. Some, I'm sure, would be more comfortable if I'd stuck to a set of black-and-white criteria. But I believe fiction is best served by trusting your instincts, so that's what I tried to do.

Many of the things I learned in putting this collection together didn't seem to fit into the book anywhere. They're the impressions gathered from talking to so many writers and editors, the places I found where the vastly different experiences and backgrounds of all these people meet.

Some of the things I learned didn't surprise me. I heard a chorus of voices echoing every creative writing teacher and how-to book in the world, proving that some basics are indeed basic: To succeed as a writer you have to read and read and read. You have to keep writing. You have to be open to criticism. You have to research the markets for your work, keep your stories out there no matter how often you're rejected, and recognize there's a large element of chance in what gets accepted.

What I found more interesting were the common threads in what the editors and writers had to say about how they work. The most striking of those threads is something everyone had trouble putting into words. They talked about how important it is to get to know yourself, to trust yourself, to write from your own personal well of emotion. Sally Herrin said it like this: "You have to know who you are and how you perceive life. You won't know what you mean unless you listen to what you say." Abraham Rodriguez said, "I could talk your ear off about any number of social conditions, but when it comes to writing, it's all about deep-down feelings. It's just my life, it's just what I know."

As they talked about that personal side of writing, the writers and editors showed me the process is private and sometimes painful; it is gut-level. It is also unexplainable. "Where did the story itself come from?" Richard Plant said, "That's tricky. Where *do* stories originate?" But it is essential, that much is clear, and every writer has to find the place where his or her stories come from and then trust that place.

Writing that comes from the writer's depths, several people said, is universal. It touches emotional truths that go beyond the specifics of the story. Eileen Schnurr said, "What we're really looking for is something that speaks to you in a very human way—an interesting and intelligent human way—and talks about universal concerns, giving you some insight, making you live something that you haven't, and so awaken ideas and understanding in your mind." Bob Shar of the *Crescent Review* said, "Too many stories don't transcend the situation. They're sort of insular."

Many of the editors tried to translate all that into some specifics. They said they want stories that don't rely on artificial tricks or techniques, stories that show movement and resolution.

"At the *Atlantic,* our preference is for stories, as distinct from sketches or cross-sections of life or glimpses of how things are," C. Michael Curtis told me. "We get an awful lot of very good and elegant writing in which not very much happens, or if it happens, it doesn't move very much toward some sort of conclusion."

"The finely crafted stories are nice to read, but when you put them down, they're gone," Shar said. "The stories that stick in your mind when you're through are the ones you go back to."

Endings, in particular, seem to cause a lot of trouble. Too many writers don't have them. "They don't end it in a satisfying sort of resolution because it seems to be sort of pat," Schnurr said. "So they leave you sort of in the middle of nowhere." She calls these the "suddenly he felt tired" endings. "This is a real problem—how to end a story satisfactorily without being simple or trite or just saying it straight out," she said. "This is one of the difficulties of writing, but it has to be dealt with."

Two other points were often repeated. First, editors are not the enemy. Every editor I talked to said editing is done in cooperation with the author, and only one writer admitted to feeling at all pressured by an editor. "One thing writers should realize is that editors are their friends," Jay Schaefer of *Fiction Network* said. "We're not out to steal or gut or otherwise destroy the creative effort. We *need* writers; we need stories for our magazines."

Comments and suggestions from an editor should be welcome, the editors said. "Any ink you get about a story is a good sign," Cecelia Hagen of the *Northwest Review* said. "We wouldn't bother unless we felt the story had some promise."

The second point is that beginning writers are at no disadvantage. "They're treated absolutely the same way as more established writers," Maura High of *New England Review and Bread Loaf Quarterly* said. "I distrust resumes." Schaefer agreed. "We depend on finding new writers. It's actually the point of what we're doing. The better known writers can always get published. We're looking for new voices."

Even the editors of commercial magazines agreed. Almost every major glossy nominated stories for this collection (*Redbook, Seventeen, Playboy, Cosmopolitan, McCall's, Omni,* to name a few) and most nominated more than one. I found no evidence that new writers are treated differently at the commercial magazines than at literary magazines, though of course the odds of getting published are longer at the bigger magazines. (The *Atlantic* gets 12,000 submissions a year.)

But ignore the odds and keep on writing, all the editors said. Richard Peabody of *Gargoyle* said, "I've rejected some people seventy-five times and then taken a story from them. They just kept at it until they got it right."

But I've kept you long enough. You should be reading the stories, not reading about them. So I'll do my thank-you's and let you get to them.

First, let me thank the authors who shared themselves with me so openly. Their candor and enthusiasm have contributed as much to the world of fiction as have their wonderful stories. I know we'll hear more from them.

All the editors who worked with me, whether or not their magazines are represented here, are due a large measure of gratitude for recognizing and nurturing good writing. They get so little credit for so difficult a job. I'm glad they shared some of its rewards with me.

Jean Fredette at Writer's Digest Books, both editor and friend, gave me the support and freedom I needed to do this. I'm not sure we always saw things the same way, but she trusted me and believed in this idea. Her guidance and encouragement were invaluable.

I N T R O D U C T I O N

. . . .

9

And Howard Wells did so much more than help choose the stories. He was sounding board and critic, a wellspring of ideas and support; my mainstay. This is, truly, a product of mutuality.

Linda S. Sanders
February 15, 1989

Sister

I am on the cool green grass when Sister comes rolling in the driveway. Her husband is driving and when the car stops, Sister grabs the car keys and throws them to the grass. "He's pounded my legs all the way here," she cries and Daddy comes down from the porch. Sister is sobbing now and her babies are in the back seat with two brown bags of groceries, moving around as if in slow motion, rolling their fingers around their faces, and breathing tiny spots of steam on the windows. Sister is still crying and I—with my good eye for shiny objects—find the keys and carry them back, using my index finger as a hook for the thick silver ring.

Daddy is talking to Sister's husband like nothing ever happened. Talking about the heat and the dry dusty air. I lean my head in the baby blue car and look down to Sister's lap; she is wrapped in a flimsy cotton dress and sure enough, all along her knee, round bruises have bunched themselves together like a cluster of old grapes, soft and tender.

The gravel driveway snaps under my pink plastic flip-flops. I am just tall enough to reach my bony arm in front of Sister and dangle the keys like bells in between her and her man, just tall and brave enough, and he grabs those keys and stares at Sister like she is a moving dartboard, and he is intent on making his point. I move away and Sister pushes open her door and pulls away from his grabbing hand. She runs across the lawn and her man jumps out of the car and follows her. He is taking long giant steps behind Sister. He grabs her hair which is short and has no give, he grabs it tight and drops her down on her back. His arm comes down like a half-moon and his fist bangs her face. "Oh," I hear the wind push out of her and Daddy moves toward them hollering, "Lydia, get out here."

Mama comes out of the house waving her white dish cloth in the air. "No," she screams, "not in my yard, not my girl." She runs to them, then stops and puts her hands on her hips. Her bigness makes Sister's man look small. "No," she says firm-like.

Sister stands up and the blood spits out like a red waterfall. She covers her face and walks funny. Daddy turns away and goes into the house, his whole body drooping like a wet rag. The girl baby starts to cry—wide open-mouthed cries—and everyone looks toward the car and they are all quiet on the sunburnt lawn. Then Sister's man makes his move. He runs to the car and drives away. The babies' faces look like melted masks against the windows. When their car pulls away, things are unusually close and quiet. We watch them until all that is left is a swirling circle of powder over the parched road and Sister begins to cry, not a likely cry, but a cry like a moose's call, all whiny and low.

In the night, I wake tossing and crying because I feel crowded in my sleep. The day's heat is still trapped under my skin. I hear a train roll by two or three fields away and I listen until I can hear no more whistle. The silence blends in just right with my brother's wheezing; he sleeps in the hallway outside my door. I move to the window and play with the dark curl that hides on the back of my neck. Clover smell is rushing around outside and I push my face against the black screen to breathe a deeper breath. I think, "Oh, Sister, I hope your face is okay. I hope your man learns to keep his temper down." I watch the fireflies that cover the fields and light on and off like snow sparkles. I watch the fields and heavens, flies and stars, all bright, first one, then the other and I say, "Jesus, don't blame me for giving those keys. I don't want Sister here, Jesus. . . ." Brother wheezes louder. Wheezy Weasel, I call him when his chest gets heavy. I go to him and he is fast asleep. His eyes cross furiously under his thin lids. I whisper his name. His front teeth rest on his fat bottom lip. "Wheezy," I say, "get up quick, the whole world's on fire."

On Sunday Wheezy is sicker than ever. His face swells red and Mama puts a mustard pack on his chest and head until his entire bed and body stains yellow. Mama hums him a hymn. She's humming *Glory Glory Hallelujah*. She sings it over and over until my brother says, "Mama." He lifts his head and he says, "Mama, please no more." Mama stops her singing right up quick and sends me away. I go down the crooked steps and walk to where Daddy sits on the porch. His face is as long and as brown as an Indian's. He and Sister are talking about getting the babies back. Daddy is whittling a man's head out of a smooth piece of wood. There are thin white shavings dropping between his shoes. I go out to the grass where I have worn a patch from sitting. I sit in that patch and watch the ghosts of dandelions blow through the air until Mama comes and gets me for church.

We walk down the dusty road and Mama's presence is as big as the sun itself. She says Daddy will take care of things at home. She says my brother is feeling better. Her skin is as white and thin as papier mache and I wish I could smell like her, all clean and freshly brushed with dusting powder.

The touch of Mama's cool hand as I lie across her lap during the sermon comforts me. The preacher's voice is soft, but the *amens* echo around us like gunfire. "Amen," I say under my breath as I chew the thumbnail which I have saved especially for this time alone with Mama. Even now, we are not really alone. Even now, I share Mama with her interest in what's being said.

When we get home, Sister and her babies are on the porch with Daddy. You can tell by the way they are sitting that they are not discussing anything important. The babies stick their faces out through the slats of the railing and chew at the wood. Wheezy sits on the porch step all covered with dry mustard; his eyes are like green marbles in the sun. Mama checks his face for fever and pats the top of his head. I sit down beside him, twisting my hair around my fingers.

"Mama," Sister says, "Daddy went and got the babies back. He says there was nothing to it 'cause their father was laid out cold on the couch." She says this very proud of Daddy, and Mama picks up one of the babies and looks into its face. Mama clicks her tongue and the baby smiles.

"Mama, I just gotta move back home. I can't take being scared all the time. I gotta get me and the babies out of that trailer before he kills us," Sister says. "Mama, can I come back home?"

Daddy stands up. He looks out over the lawn and taps the whittled man's head against the railing, then walks down to the old well house, which is no longer a well house, but a storage space for his beer bottles. Daddy is not bad, he only drinks when things get too much for him, bills or my brother's wheezes. Sister sits up and watches Mama's face. She is as alert and nervous as a caged dog. "Mama?" she snaps.

"You know we got nothing extra," Mama says and Sister begins this long plea. Twisting her voice to match her words and saying she'll sleep on the floor, she won't eat much, she'll do anything just to get away from *him*. I shrink into my body when I hear her talk about staying forever. I think how Mama will be all tied up with Wheezy and Sister and her babies, and how Daddy will stay drunk, and I'll be nothing. I'll be the shriveled up pea in the corner of the pod. I think how Sister is like a long sticky fly-catch blowing in the wind and we are all the flies sticking to her troubles.

"What about your Daddy?" Mama says. "You know he hasn't had any work for a month." She bounces the baby in her arms, up and down, swaying her hips like she's in a hula hoop.

"I'll do Tupperware parties and I'll pay rent," Sister says looking big-eyed like she has already had a glimpse of her new life.

Mama takes the baby into the kitchen and the screen door bangs behind her. Sister picks up her other baby and balances him on her hip bone.

"Can I or can't I?" she asks and Mama says something back that makes the worried lines go out of Sister's face.

The door of the well house is slightly open and the cool from the darkness pushes out. There are empty brown bottles all along the walls and it takes my eyes a while to adjust without the sun. Daddy is sitting in one corner with a piece of hay dangling from his mouth. When he drinks, the hay remains in his mouth, unchanged. I sit down in the opposite corner beside an old milk can and roll an empty around the palms of my hand. "Well, I guess she's gonna stay," I say and Daddy just watches me and drinks. When he guzzles, his adam's apple bobs in and out like a horse's heartbeat. I stare down at the musty floor boards. Mama says Daddy drinks because his soul is troubled. She also says if we could see our soul we'd see that it is in the shape of wings and I believe her, because sometimes when I sit on the lawn and stare out at the green mountain ridges that surround our home, I can feel my soul wanting to get loose to see what lies beyond those high slopes. Daddy chugs a whole beer before he sees my thumb stuck in the top of the beer bottle. The thumb is swelling blue from my tugging to get it out. "What in hell?" Daddy staggers over toward me. He grabs my arm and smashes the bottle against the old milk can. The brown glass makes a sharp obstacle course all around me and I struggle with words in my throat, but they don't come up. Daddy pushes me out into the light. "Get out," he says and slams the door behind me.

I know Daddy's anger with me is just the beginning of things to come with Sister being around. I wander down the long road and take a turn at the crossing toward the old folk's home that Mama calls heaven's waiting room. I stop at the black bridge and let my feet hang out over the edge and stare down where the clear creek water rushes by like a jet. I can see the round rocks in the creek's bottom and I wonder about my kazoo. I wonder if maybe it's hidden between those rocks getting all rusty. I dropped it over when I was thinking about a boy and Mama would probably say that was good punishment for me. His name is Lenny Moore and he's the only boy in the whole fourth grade. He sits at the desk in front of me. He's jiggly and nervous, and he's always sending me scrawly notes about how he likes me and would like to kiss me someday, and for a while I liked the notes and the thoughts I had of Lenny. I liked him a lot up until the day he accidentally wet his pants and his yellow water ran back under his chair to my new white sneakers. It's hard to forget that smell and the yellow stains and besides the rest of the kids call him Leaky Moore, which keeps us both cringing and blushing at the memory. The smell of melting tar comes out around the dark boards of the bridge, and the smell is so strong you'd think it came in a black cloud. I swing my legs and forget about my thumb and Daddy and all the broken glass, but I still have a clear picture of Sister and her babies.

At the old folk's home, I crawl up on Mrs. Harris's bed and rest myself. Her room smells of plastic and fly repellent. She is wandering around the room touching all her things and saying, "I've got to get ready, I've got to get ready." Mama's been letting me come to visit Mrs. Harris all summer and she is always like this, not quite sure of where she belongs anymore. She says her old man sleeps up in the attic and bakes molasses cookies all day. She says the mosquitos sneak in through her screen at night and bite her to death. I tell Mrs. Harris there is no screen on the window, but she just keeps on talking and smiling like I've never said a word. She takes some old crochet work out of a plastic bag and rubs her wrinkled fingers over it. I tell her all about the gall of Sister and her babies, and she is so happy for me, having family and all, and she puts the crochet work back in the bag, sniffing and trying to hide her sad joy. Before I leave, Mrs. Harris combs the snarls from my hair. She combs it one hundred times and I count the mosquito bites on her legs which are really too many to count.

On the way home I find Daddy wading around in the creek. He is pushing his legs against the current and staring down through the water in a panic. I lean out over the water as far as I dare and I say, "Daddy, what are you doing?" He looks up, his mouth all wilted and opened and he squints his eyes at me. He screams my name and his scream bounces under the bridge and back to the water. He rubs his face, then slaps at the current like he's disgusted. He whispers my name, all worn out.

Daddy takes me home by the arm and his wet self makes spots of mud on the dirt road. He hangs on to my arm like he's afraid I'll get away, like I'm some shiny slippery trout and I know what he thinks. He's thinking back to the black bridge. He's thinking that I might have been lying under the water, still, and in another world. He's thinking it over and over.

We're almost home and I can see Mama standing in the doorway wagging the fly swatter and I know what I'm in for. Daddy keeps pulling me along and when we step on the porch, Mama takes one big step toward us. She grabs my arm and I begin to circle around her like a human Maypole. "Don't *slap* you *slap* ever *slap* go *slap* away *slap* without *slap* telling *slap* us *slap* where *slap* you're *slap* going *SLAP SLAP.*" I run upstairs to my room and bury my wet face in the feather pillow and for a long time I don't look at the red marks on my legs.

When Mama wakes me, the sun has gone down. She takes me into her room where everyone except Daddy is sitting in the dark on the bed. They are listening to the voice in the yard. Sister says her man is as drunk as a hoot. His words are running all together like unsettled Jell-O. "Give me my babies, I want my kids back. Give 'em back or I'll shoot all of you. I'll blow you all to kingdom come." Things get real still and you can feel the fear running through each of us as if we were all hanging on to an electric fence. I can feel it pushing right out to the end of my fingers. Wheezy is shaking like a dried up leaf and just to watch him makes me shake. Sister wraps one arm around me and I think about the story Daddy tells about the crazy man who went to a farmer's house and shot his whole family while they slept. Daddy said he'd never seen such a sight, all those bodies bled dry in their beds. I can see us all slumped over in this bed in a pool of blood, and right away everything that I've thought or felt these last few days seems stupid.

We hear the screen door slam and Mama moves to the hall window. I go right behind her. Sister's man is sitting on the hood of his car with a bottle in one hand and a gun in the other. He's loose and wiry like a Slinky toy. Daddy stands right in front of him. I close my eyes. "Give me the gun," Daddy says. "Go home and get yourself sober." There is a tiny little click and then stillness like the whole world has disappeared. I open my eyes and Sister's man points the gun right at Daddy's chest. Mama and I both pull our breath back through our mouths in a gasp. And Daddy reaches out and takes the gun from him in one clean sweep, smooth as honey, and Mama says, "Put the babies to bed." Sister's man rolls himself into a ball. He says he has lost everything and starts to cry. He cries so hard and so loud that I believe he is crying for all of us. It seems like all of our hurts have snuck down inside of him and are now pouring out on the top of his car in tears and wet noises.

Later, Daddy comes into my room and looks down at me and Sister's baby. The baby has its face shoved into the mattress and is sound asleep. Daddy makes a moon shadow across my white sheets. He says he wanted to make sure the bed is big enough for the baby and me. I say it is. Daddy is just one big dark spot in the middle of my room. He drops his hand down and I touch it. I feel the red metal of my kazoo hidden away in his palm like a lost treasure. Daddy doesn't say anything, he just lets the kazoo go and goes back to his room. I blow it once to see if it still works and the girl baby turns and snuggles up to my side. Her breath is sour and small and wispy. I listen to it go in and out of her like clockwork and I imagine the flapping of wings around me, in the night.

Notes

In Deborah Joy Corey's "Sister," one single detail almost broke my heart. The little girl who tells the story trots off to church to steal a moment alone with her mother. She describes the service like this:

The touch of Mama's cool hand as I lie across her lap during the sermon comforts me. The preacher's voice is soft, but the *amens* echo around us like gunfire. "Amen," I say under my breath as I chew the thumbnail which I have saved especially for this time alone with Mama. Even now, we are not really alone. Even now, I share Mama with her interest in what's being said.

That thumbnail did it. I don't know why—perhaps because I was a nail-biter too. Or perhaps because I spent many, many Sunday mornings in church lying across my own mother's lap. It doesn't matter. What *does* matter is the way details like that one can reach out from the page.

Corey uses those details sparingly but effectively in "Sister." She gives you a specific, concrete detail and then uses it to pull you bodily into the world she's created. Pink plastic flip-flops snapping against gravel. A man's adam's apple bobbing in and out as he drinks beer from a brown bottle. The smell of plastic and fly repellent at an old folks' home. The *slap* of a fly swatter hitting a little girl's bare legs.

Corey's feeling for detail is obvious even when she talks about writing the story. " 'Sister' came to me in the early morning," she remembers. "I was living by the ocean then and a storm was whipping up on the water, the window panes were rattling, and I had my head covered in the bed."

The story came to her in complete sentences, in what felt like a poem, Corey says. She, too, was moved by the details. "I immediately fell in love with 'Sister' and when the words *all along her knee, round bruises have bunched themselves together like a cluster of old grapes, soft and tender* came, I began to cry and reached under my bed for a notepad and pen."

But it takes more than a few well-chosen details to make a good short story. The details have to add up to something. For John J. Clayton, former fiction editor of the *Agni Review,* stories had to have two things to get published. "We were looking for fiction that (1) isn't afraid to express *heart,* and (2) has a quality of *mysterious fullness.*"

He explains heart like this: "There's no hip deadness, emotional blankness—which is, I think, psychological defense posing as post-modern style." He prefers stories that "aren't afraid to express yearning or the pain of loss or tenderness or fear."

Fullness is a bit harder to pin down. Clayton sees it in stories that "vibrate out beyond surface conflicts and continue to vibrate after the story is done. It's their mystery, their strange fullness, that give them life."

Those two qualities are why he chose "Sister" to be included in the last issue of *Agni* he edited before turning the magazine back over to founder Askold Melnyczuk.

Clayton says that when he began to read "Sister" he was "hooked by the narrator's voice. It's lyrical and still ordinary. It's never false."

But as he kept reading, he began to respond to the characters. He says he is amazed at how much Corey is able to convey in a short story. "She's able to make me care, to feel the pain and desires not only of the narrator but of the father, the abused sister, the mother—feel them and take them into myself."

One reason Corey is able to get so much across is that use of detail. Clayton says, "She's able to suggest intense, complex inner states through the use of *things*—images in the actions and in metaphor that express the drama, express what's going on in the characters' hearts, express the *meaning* of the story."

An example of the way Corey uses something concrete to convey something emotional, Clayton says, is how she shows us the father's reaction to his older daughter's plight. "He doesn't *think about* his daughter's abusive husband. He whittles a man's head out of wood, then we hear he's gone to get the babies back."

That scene parallels the closing one, Clayton says. "At the end, his tenderness toward his daughter is powerfully expressed not by talking about it, but by handing back her kazoo in the dark room.

That ending makes me hold my breath."

For her part, Corey says she doesn't know what makes a good story. "But I think that it may have something to do with a lot of waiting and listening," she says. "Some of my stories seem to write themselves in another place and then come fully formed for me to put on paper—those are the stories I trust the most—others are more work and sometimes not as rewarding."

She says "Sister" was one of the stories she trusts. It came in a complete draft within hours, beginning with the first sentence, which Corey heard herself say aloud. "My voice was more slack than usual and the words did not come from inside me, but seemed to float from somewhere outside, as if on the wind," she recalls.

Perhaps because of how it came to her, Corey talks about her story very personally, even refers to it as "she." "When I read her again, there are still some words that I would change and perhaps I would make better use of white space," she says. "Maybe that is because I read her as a stranger. This story still has a way of surprising me and I guess that is where my love for writing manifests itself. Like any good thing in life, it is familiar yet so full of the unknown."

Corey made a few minor changes after the first draft and began sending it out. It was rejected five times before Clayton said yes. Corey says that when Clayton called, she thought he was a friend playing a joke. After all, the story "had not been in the mail very long. I have one story that has been out thirty-nine times," she says.

Once she realized the call was legitimate, she was pleased. "To have an editor choose your work reinforces positively what you spend your life doing," she says. But she tried to keep the acceptance in perspective. "I don't think getting published is necessary to validate you as a writer. The work is what counts."

Corey says some of her family and friends don't acknowledge her writing. She thinks fear is part of it—particularly for those who wonder where her fictional characters come from. "I would like to say, in defense of my characters, there is a bit of my father in all of my fathers, a bit of my mother in all of my mothers, and a bit of my sister in all of my sisters, but for the most part, they are imagined characters and free to be what they want to be."

She says fear is part of writing, too. "I don't think Kerouac wrote *On the Road* in one sitting because he was a genius. I think he was afraid that if he stopped, the voice he had captured might not be there when he returned. I have been paralyzed by that fear myself and have on a few occasions even glanced through the want ads."

It is not likely that Corey will give up writing, though. "When fear happens," she says, "you have to remember that nothing matches the feeling of being inspired, when your pen can't move fast enough for the words."

A Tale of Fashion

Y ou men won't like this, bless your hearts. Fashion does make most of you yawn, admit it. Already, I can see your noses turning up and that flat, glazed look of put-upon boredom rolling down over your eyes. Hey, pretend like you're watching a sequence of sheer stockings sliding down a chorus line's legs in a television commercial. Can you hear the sound of all that hot nylon parting from those sweaty gams? Whoosh, whoosh, whoosh, over the knees, past the ankles, off the toes. Then, a giant unanimous sigh of relief: the feeling of cramped piggies freed from a long night's labor. Heavens, wiggle those little soldiers until they almost sing from the cool joy of it all. I'll try to keep your interest, boys.

My brother used to read *Cosmopolitan,* for the pictures, he said. My sisters and I knew he was secretly checking out the new makeup shades and reading the advice columns. He'd become flustered and start barking out voyeur noises—Ooh, baby! What a body!—when one of us happened upon him with his face buried in the slick pages. Then, he'd sling the magazine on the floor, walk to the refrigerator and yank it open, pull the tab off a can of beer, drink it in one long swallow, belch, and scratch his stomach. We ignored his fake-out; we're not dummies. Through the years, he was our number one fashion critic and love-lorn advisor. We never left the house for any destination of romantic potential without checking our appearances and attitudes with him. He never let us down, bless his heart.

Lavender lace lingerie, black patent leather spike heels, gold lamé evening bags, hand-carved ivory combs, diamond and platinum bracelets, fire-and-ice lipstick, topaz dinner rings, silky sandalwood dusting powder, pearlized pink fingernail polish, Russian sable jackets, red silk cocktail dresses: none of those items are included in this story. This is a story about muumuus.

I play hell getting those women to wear them. Some articles of clothing are so hideous that one cannot with a straight face say, "Here, put this on." That's the situation with the muumuus. The saga of the muumuu is one of decline; once, they were worn by sassy, smiling, Hawaiian mamas who sang love songs and wove beautiful leis from pampas grass and orchids. The garments were bright and flowing, leaving plenty of room for the love handles acquired during all of those pig roasts. They looked good, cheerfully garish, in the island sunshine. Then, some wicked designer from Seventh Avenue went to Honolulu on vacation. The rest is history.

Fat and tacky women everywhere adopted the native fashion, allowing merchants to unload the worldwide surplus of double-knit polyester and iridescent floral print rayon blend. The kind that snags. I'm telling you those dresses are ugly.

The craze passed and was supplanted by a craving for Dale Evans costumes; thousands of the muumuus choked Goodwill bins across the country and piled up in glow-in-the-dark stacks in the corners of D.A.V. stores. Few humans are forced to look at the muumuus anymore.

Oh, yes, I've worn one of those muumuus. I'm usually a very snappy dresser but it was a special occasion.

The exam room was packed, standing-room only. Aside from me, the star of the show, the crowd was made up of the elderly hospital chaplain who wore a toupee and spaghetti sauce stains on his tie; a hassled-looking nurse wearing running shoes and a hot-pink stethoscope around her neck, and two police officers—a pug-nosed, squat-bodied rookie and a no-baloney veteran of the night shift. There was also a middle-aged doctor whose football-shaped beer belly flopped over the waistband of his designer jeans. In the corner stood a polished police lieutenant who wore sharp musk cologne and two marksmanship medals; next to me, between the table and the wall, was the rape counselor. She was eyeing the cops and the doctor like they were about to gang up on me.

I was afraid that there wouldn't be enough oxygen in the small space to supply all of our lungs; I had to stop myself from gasping for air. Only the rape counselor and the chaplain were partially successful in camouflaging their boredom. I was fascinated with the lieutenant and he knew it.

He was leaning against the counter, his pelvis angled out to accommodate all the equipment hanging from his belt, and the official expression of concerned interest that covered his face kept slipping, like an old Halloween mask with rotten elastic. I was trying to keep my mind on the little rookie with his tiny spiral notebook and his interesting questions—So, have you ever been out on a date with the perpetrator?—but my eyes wouldn't leave the lieutenant for very long. I glanced away for a second, when I looked back he was gazing fondly at his reflection in the shiny metal paper-towel holder. He reached up and touched his hair, carefully patting it into place. Then, he rewarded himself for being such a good-looking devil by busting out in an evil, sexy grin. The rape counselor followed my gaze and then she poked him in the ribs; I wanted to tell him to go ahead and slobber all over the metal, but the door flew open and my attention was diverted. Two detectives elbowed into the room; they didn't try to hide their yawns.

I sat there in the muumuu and sniffed the odor rising from the bright tartan plaid fabric. I wasn't sure if it was Evening in Paris or Vicks Vaporub; there were some subtle undertones of permanent wave solution and stale sweat. The detectives pulled the muumuu up above my breasts and positioned me like a Playmate of the Month; I had to hold my arms up over my head with my hands clasped together while they snapped pictures of my bruises. The lieutenant watched with a slightly higher level of interest than he had displayed before, and I watched him as he rested his palm on the butt of his revolver.

Now, I'm a rape counselor. The worst part of my job is trying to talk the victims into putting on those damn muumuus. Some kindly soul hauls them over from the junk clothing store in big bundles; each emergency room has a box full of the things. You see, the cops take away the victim's clothes, or her bedsheet, or her shower curtain—whatever she has on when she makes her way to the hospital. I was wearing an orange chenille bedspread, toga-fashion. It was originally my grandmother's and I hated it; I'm glad that the police took it away.

Whatever the woman has draped over her bones is confiscated, usually by me, and stuffed into a big paper bag. The bag is labeled with her name and the date. That bag goes into a larger clear plastic bag with the rest of the artifacts. A run-of-the-mill, weeknight rape would probably generate the following debris: one vial with a few drops of saliva in the bottom, a few plucked—not cut, the roots must be identifiable—pubic hairs, two tubes of blood, four or five vaginal smears and swabs, the all-important sperm motility count, and the pictures. Photographs of her rope burns or lacerations or knife pricks. I kept one copy of my favorite bite-mark picture; you can hardly see the scars on my neck, now. On a summer Saturday night there might be a few extras—shiny pieces of silver tape that have been slowly eased off her lips, x-rays of her facial fractures, or a length of her phone cord. Anyway, it's sayonara to her body coverings, off they go to the evidence locker to grow mold. The detectives always make sure that I poke a few small holes in the bags to let some air in and stave off the inevitable decay. They say that the smell could knock down five strong men when the evidence is unwrapped, usually months later, if ever, in a courtroom. I try to do my part to keep those guys off the floor, bless their hearts.

After the poking and prodding, the plucking and pelvic exam, the pitying and pledges of immediate police action, my moment arises. I begin to educate the woman about life. In my training sessions, when I was learning to become a rape counselor, the instructor said that most women will use the rape as a time marker. Like high school graduation, only more so. The recently raped woman will think in terms of before and after; her life will be cut into two segments, two sensibilities. Trust and terror. Most women don't know that they're doing this; it didn't dawn on me until the instructor pointed it out. But I did think that way; B.R. and A.R. Safety and survival.

Those muumuus really make my job tough. I'm bent on getting those women back on the street, back to the grocery store, back to work. Back to life. I insist that they recognize their own power—their ability to pull in another breath. I am merciless; no sniveling allowed. They are alive and I beat them over the heads with it. No use letting that yellow-bellied throwback, that cretinous pervert, that acid ice-pick of a rapist continue to rape you over and over again. I just won't allow it.

I came home, to the scene of the crime, and sat in the dark for three days. Shaking. Sobbing. Blubbering all over myself. Then, I brushed my teeth and ate a box of saltine crackers. My neck hurt like hell. I couldn't feel anything from the collarbones down. I slept for a week. Finally, I staggered from the couch and looked in the mirror. What was the first thing I saw? You guessed it: that painfully horrid, rick-rack-festooned, plaid muumuu. There were two stiff pieces of kleenex in the pocket. I went back to the couch and slept for another week. How could I let him do that to me? Almost three weeks as a plaid vegetable. A rick-rack victim of fashion and self-pity. I should've been out learning karate or how to assemble and fire an M-16. The animal raped three more women while I reclined, rotting, in my dark living room. That piece of news blasted me off of my couch.

That muumuu had made me a victim for too long.

If I had it my way, there would be a room full of fresh, brand-new, soft, and gorgeous clothes; the women could go in and pick out whatever they wanted to wear. Someone would wash their hair for them and dry it and they would look beautiful. There would be plenty of hot water so they could take as many showers as they wanted; the towels would be thick and fluffy; the soap would leave them as clean as vanilla ice cream. Someone would rub scented potions on their sore necks; the pain would vanish. Feathery fingers would massage their temples and remove all of the fear from their minds. Their muscles would glow with strength and bravery and pride. There would be crystal atomizers of perfume and great cut glass vases of roses all over the place. There would be brandy and smelling salts; a beige brocade fainting couch would sit in the corner, draped with a pale pink angora afghan. There would be old-fashioned lace hankies to cry in and someone would hold their hands and say, "It's all right," over and over again. It would be kind of a cross between a funeral parlor and a fantastic boudoir.

Then, they would be restored. They would go into the next room, wearing their new clothes, their self-respect resurrected and their backbones fortified with steely resolve, and learn how to kill a man at close range.

Notes

Maura High, editor of the *New England Review and Bread Loaf Quarterly,* is talking about why she liked "A Tale of Fashion" almost immediately. She reads the first sentence aloud, drawing it out slowly: "You men won't like this, *bless your hearts.*" She pauses. "Isn't that lovely? It issues a sort of challenge—'You men won't like this'—and then becomes rather charming—'bless your hearts.' "

That, she says, is one of the strengths of Jeanmarie Epperly's story. It provokes strong emotions, then immediately challenges those emotions, bouncing the reader around from one reaction to another. "It's almost a rape of the reader," High says.

High says Epperly keeps up that one-two punch throughout the story. The title, for instance, evokes a soft, homespun image with the word *tale,* then contradicts that image with the word *fashion,* which conveys glamour. The third paragraph lulls you with a long, rhythmic list of luxurious fashion items, then says abruptly, "None of those items are included in this story. This is a story about muumuus." The following paragraphs make you laugh, with their references to "iridescent floral print rayon blend" and "glow-in-the-dark stacks in the corners of D.A.V. stores," then smack you with the information that the narrator was once raped.

High also points out the paragraph where the narrator describes her fascination with the police lieutenant. It begins, "He was leaning against the counter, his pelvis angled out to accommodate all the equipment hanging from his belt. . . ." For an instant, High says, she found herself thinking that perhaps this was a loose woman, one who couldn't keep her eyes off men even in the worst of circumstances. Then, as she saw the officer's obvious boredom and infatuation with his own image in the shiny paper-towel holder, she recoiled, thinking, "How could I think that?"

Epperly knows the reader is, in her words, "kind of getting punched around emotionally." She once read the story aloud and watched the listeners' reactions when the narrator said, "Oh, yes, I've worn one of those muumuus."

"They'd been laughing up to that point, and then all of a sudden they felt terrible that they'd been laughing. I knew I had them then."

The story is able to pull off that effect because of the narrator, who Epperly says is an unstable character. She says the narrator couldn't be an outsider, someone like a nurse, and still convey the strong emotions necessary. That's why she made her a rape victim.

"I wanted her anger, and her empathy with the people she worked with," Epperly says. "I wanted the anger to be witnessed without it being diluted."

High agrees that the narrator is crucial to this story. "The language and the structure aren't just strategies in this story. They're consistent with the narrator. The author doesn't play a line for laughs or just for effect; it's all keyed to the narrator's mood and her anger."

Epperly, who works in the emergency room of a Wichita hospital, says rape is very difficult to write about, in part because the emotions connected with it are so strong. She does, in fact, have to hand rape victims ugly muumuus to wear and sees the turmoil the women go through. "They are so frightened," she says. "The fear is on almost a cellular level."

Epperly says she's pleased with two other aspects of the story in addition to the narrator. One is the effect of the focus on muumuus. "It makes it [the humiliation] a real thing—something the readers can feel and see," she says.

The other is the ending. In the original version the ending "wasn't as hard core. It wimped out at the end," Epperly says. When she revised the story before sending it to High, she created the fantasy where the narrator explains how she'd like rape victims to be treated.

While she didn't know the ending was new when she accepted the story, High says the fantasy is important to the story. "There is a real resolution. She brings it all together in the end. Often beginning writers don't resolve their stories—whether they think it's fashionable not to or simply don't know how to write an ending, I don't know—but it's one of the things we look for in a story."

Epperly wrote "A Tale of Fashion" in a little more than an hour and the first place she sent it was to High's magazine.

But the process wasn't as easy as it sounds, Epperly says. She had long been troubled by the pain and humiliation of the rape victims she treated and had thought about how to write about those feelings, but couldn't find the right approach.

One night, working the overnight shift, she cared for a woman who had been raped in "an especially degrading manner." So when Epperly got home, she sat down and began writing. The story came quickly then, but the inspiration was grounded in several months of thought and three years of writing other stories, as well as five years of writing poetry.

"Everything I did up to that point was part of getting that story written," Epperly says. "All of it is behind that story."

Although Epperly had been writing stories for three years and sending them out—and even says "A Tale of Fashion" isn't the best story she's ever written—she'd never been published before. She says that after a writer has reached a certain level of writing, getting published may depend on reaching the right editor at the right time. "I think it's a game of chance, I really do," she says.

So when the letter from High arrived, she was surprised. "I was screaming," she says. "I was very happy and very shocked."

The story went through very little editing before it appeared—High says she sometimes works very closely with authors to bring out the potential in a story, but that this one needed almost no work.

After the story appeared, Epperly says, the reaction from readers was strong. "I have received so much mail about this story it's incredible," she says. The story was reprinted in a college newspaper after a woman was attacked on campus, and other authors who appeared in the same issue of the New England Review wrote to encourage her as a new writer.

Some of the strongest reaction has come from men, who tell her the story gave them new insight into rape. At the public reading, Epperly says, women reacted to the story almost immediately but men seemed to spend time thinking about it first.

Either reaction makes Epperly happy. The real strength of her story, she says simply, is, "It affects people."

Way to the Dump

Zuerner was breaking away from the Boston meeting to come to the Cape, but surely not because of a casual invitation extended in a passing encounter with Elligott a year ago. The two men disliked each other for no particular reason, the most incurable kind of aversion; Elligott's invitation emerged for want of something better to say; neither he nor Zuerner had expected it to be taken up. Even so, Zuerner had telephoned and asked if it would be convenient if he came by.

Was the merger on again? Did they want his stock?

"Stay for lunch," Elligott had said, impulsively, and immediately regretted this sign of weakness. He never managed to get the tone right with Zuerner. He hadn't even had the presence of mind to say, "Let me look at the calendar." Not even "Let me see if Daisy can make it for lunch."

Elligott moved the slider and stepped out onto his terrace. Unlike early settlers' houses, placed with buffers between themselves and the wind, his house had been a summer shack before the alterations and had been built right there on the low bluff above the beach. Its prospect was across the steaming bay toward an awesome pink dawn. On the way out the tide had trapped his skiff in shore grass; returning, it mirrored the forested dune. Some day! Some scene! Elligott felt the exhilaration of a discoverer. He wondered what he'd have to pay to commission this view from the fellow who did the Indian marsh paintings in Derek's gallery. It would be worth a thousand dollars. First a strong week in the market, and now a day like this!

He shrugged comfortably in his new Bean sweater; it was just the thing for this chill Sunday morning in October. October—so soon. Quarter to six. Dowling would be open in . . . now fourteen minutes.

Nobody was on the water. Nobody was anywhere. Not a bird. The only sound came from a ratcheting cricket, augmented in Elligott's hearing aid. Fat with good luck, the cricket tensed toward cover, but the man's foot was too quick. Elligott felt a small startle at the confrontation, not enough to call fear—afraid of a cricket?— but it would have read on an instrument. Perhaps a blood admonition not to kill easily. He kicked the squash over the edge into the sand, leaving a stain and a twitching leg on the mortar joint. In an impulse of compassion or guilt he stepped out the twitch.

He stood for another moment at the terrace edge, bothered slightly that the new sun-room, in the nature of all new things, had estranged the house from its environment. It had happened before, and he knew now that in a few years the rugosa, creeper, poison ivy, catbrier, fox grape, beach plum, and innumerable unidentifiable wind- and bird-brought weeds fleeing upward from the salt would blur the margins of the foundation into the land, and the shingles would darken. The house would then come fully into its destiny. It was an extraordinary house.

He thought of a small boat going by and somebody looking up and saying to himself, That's Elligott, a noticeable man. You would trust your widow to Elligott. Perhaps not your wife; look at the bush of hair for a man his age and the athletic way he carries his weight. The house is suitable to the commanding view, what you would expect of a man like Elligott.

The hydrangea that he had cleverly placed below the terrace, so that its enormous plates of bloom could be seen from above, was at its fullest. The branch he had layered stood erect in full leaf, surely rooted. He had never imagined that gardening could be so pleasurable, and that he had such a hand for it. Farther below, in the narrow courses veining the grassy marsh, blue crabs fed; they were mostly big this time of year, no chicks; big as mitts, swimming to the rotten-meat bag and taking alarm too late to escape the sneaking net.

Wait till Zuerner began to net crabs down there for his lunch. That would get to him, all right. That would open his face! That would balance all accounts.

The irritation at his forced retirement which Elligott frequently waked with before they came to the Cape had been diminishing all year, and this morning it gave way completely to the anticipation of how boggling it would be to Zuerner to see, on this best of all possible days, how well he and Daisy lived.

Gone were the clubs and restaurants, the church and duty boards, where men who knew he had been pushed aside observed him. He had made known that resigning to become a consultant was his idea, but McGlynn, Andrewes, Draveau, Thompson, Zuerner—all of them and their wives—had known that his résumé circulated. He felt himself become transparent. To distance himself from his telephone he had the building agent's girl record that she was Mr. Elligott's office, and if you waited for the tone you could leave a message of any length. After an interval Elligott called back insurance agents he had never before heard of; *The Wall Street Journal* offered a trial subscription; business papers wanted ads for Consultant Service Indexes; somebody wanted his cousin Lewis Elligott.

And one day Daisy had said, "Why don't we fix up the cottage and see what living on the Cape would be like?"

A steadying wife—what a blessing.

From that came days like this. Today he wouldn't mind comparing lives with Andrewes, Zuerner, with McGlynn himself—any of them. Most of all Zuerner.

An odd feeling of emptiness seeped into him. He felt as he had after eagling the fifth at the Heights Club, a mixture of triumph and loss. He had been playing alone; nobody was there to see the two iron drop, nobody to take the burden of telling from him. The not quite convincing story was one he could slip into a conversation but couldn't *tell*. Zuerner was the man to sign your card. Zuerner's authority would authenticate Elligott's life to McGlynn, Andrewes, all of them at Elligott Barge & Dredge.

He decided to take the wagon. It hadn't been turned over all week; it would do the old girl good to have hot oil in her cylinders and valves. He punched the garage-door button and got in while the door complained to the top and the control panel nattered at him to put on his galoshes, comb his hair, brush his teeth, stop squinting. At The Pharmacy the *Times* would be shuffled by six. Dowling's wouldn't be busy yet; he would be able to open the paper on the counter. Be back before Daisy was even up.

The driveway crackled through the allowed disorder of scratch pines and pin oaks, bayberry and blueberry bushes, rising from the rust of pine needles. He regretted mildly that for thirty years he had let the native growth have its way when for a few dollars he could have set seedlings of better breeds that by now would have been huge, towering elegant. You could truck in hand-split shakes for the roof and Andersen windows with instant Colonial mullions and eighteen-dollar-a-square-foot tiles, but only God could make a tree. Only time marketed tall white pines. And rhododendrons like Pauley's.

He bobbed along the stony humpbacked lane kept up by the Association—PRIVATE 15 MPH PLEASE OBSERVE—and onto the state blacktop that forked at WAY TO THE DUMP, taking him toward town by the back road past Pauley's rhododendrons.

Development had not yet made progress here. The small properties were held by owners who frugally fought mortgages every percent of the way and counted on thirty bags of December scallops to help with the fuel bills. The houses had no views. The families used to grow cranberries in adjacent bogs. Cut off by barrier roads, the bogs were reduced to wetland unbuildable by law and some years away from the sort of new owners who could see the interesting tax consequences of a gift to the Conservation Fund.

But here ancestors and young marrieds had seen thickened hedges prefigured in a few sticks. He slowed while he envied the maturities. Cedars spiked in a grove of pines; lilacs that, come spring, would bear trusses above a man's reach; Pauley's rhododendrons.

Elligott knew Pauley the way he knew half a dozen building tradesmen around town; he had assumed the driver to be the man whose name was on the truck. He had called Pauley once and asked if he would work up a price on a new shower.

I'll stop next week and look at it. You near Haseley?

Elligott explained how one could easily find his place from Haseley's. He never heard from Pauley again. Par for the trades. Meanwhile, out of courtesy, Elligott waited three weeks, lost all that time before calling another plumber.

In June the rhododendrons between the road and Pauley's house had been amazing, a jungle. Maybe the bogland accounted for it. Purples, whites, reds, creams shot with yellow, ink and blood spatters. Like a park. Fifty or sixty plants must be in there, some of them giraffe-high, twenty or forty thousand dollars' worth if you had to truck them at that size and set them, and all from a few sticks. Imagining the plumber's rhododendrons transported to border his own driveway, Elligott regretted and went on.

Not a soul on the road. Not a car. Not a fisherman. Not a mass-bound Catholic.

He swung into the business-center block and parked at The Pharmacy. The business had been sold recently by heirs of the original owner, four brothers, each more famous than the next for surliness. No one had ever been said good morning to by one of these men. Downcast or elevated, each was on his way to transact troubling business; taking inventory; looking for dropped quarters, spider webs. They had sold out to a chain whose owners— some said from Worcester, some said Quincy—could distance themselves from light-bulb specials, jewelry deals, ad tabloids, senior-citizen discounts, and generic-drug propaganda. The first act of the new owners after the opening Days of Bargains was to add a dime to the price of the Sunday *Times*.

As a businessman, Elligott conceded that combination was the order of the day and that somebody had to make up the premium paid for the Going Concern—but not necessarily Paul D. Elligott. He would have taken his trade elsewhere except that The Pharmacy still employed at its cash counter a pleasant man named

Len who had overheard his name and very nearly remembered it.
It was worth a dime to have Len say, "It's Mr. Elliott. Good morning, Mr. Elliott."

"How are you today, Len?"

"Gonna make it. Will that be it? One seventy-five out of two
bills. Have a nice day, Mr. Elliott."

Twice Elligott had spelled his name in full for the *Times* reservation list, but Len's memory scan rejected such an improbable
reading. Elligott forgave him. Had he thought about it at the time,
Elligott would have written "Len" in the space on the Board of
Trade questionnaire that asked for reasons he liked to shop in
town: Good selections. Good prices. Good parking. Convenience.
Other . . . "Len."

Nevertheless, Elligott's acknowledging smile was of mea-
sured width. He recognized in himself a tendency to overcordial-
ity. One of the images of Zuerner that dripped in him like a
malfunctioning gland was the recollection of the day Zuerner had
come aboard and had been introduced around by McGlynn. Elligott had gone out to him, welcomed him warmly, braced his arm,
and gotten back—what would you call it: reserve? civility? The
face made interesting by the scarred cheek had barely ticked.

"I look forward to working with you, Elligott."

He might have been talking to a bookkeeper instead of the
vice president for corporate relations.

Zuerner's disfigurement conveyed the idea that something
extraordinary had formed him and implied that the distinction
was not only external.

Since that meeting Elligott had become increasingly aware of
a recompensing phenomenon that in time brought forward men
who had certain kinds of injury, handicap, unhandsomeness,
names—asymmetries that when they were young had kept them
down. Elligott had occasionally pointed out to people whom he
suspected of thinking he lacked independent weight that the advantage of being the namesake of the founder, even in a collateral
line, might get you in at first, but in the long run it was hardship.
Elligott sensed he would have difficulty being taken seriously

compared with a man like Zuerner, with a mark on his cheek and a bearing rehearsed to imply that he knew how to make up his mind.

In most matters whatever decision was taken, even a decision to do nothing, worked out all right if firmly asserted. Zuerner's function was to make one decision seem better than another and to identify himself in this circular way as the cause of what he was in truth an effect. McGlynn had been taken in, but not Elligott.

He thought himself wiser than Zuerner by virtue of having understood him and the power cards he played. His way of holding back to conceal his limits. His strategic unwillingness to speak early in meetings. Never answering a question if it could be turned back on the asker.

"You've given it thought. What is *your* feeling?"

"Come on, Walter," Elligott had once said, "stop the crap. Just answer the question. I'm not asking you to invest in it."

He had been certain Zuerner would retreat from such a frank challenge. But Zuerner had maintained a steady silence that made Elligott seem petulant even to himself. Involuntarily, his face repeated its recollection of Zuerner's at their first meeting, the moment watched by McGlynn, when Zuerner gained ascendancy.

At other times, when he reflected with the candor he was pleased to note in himself, Elligott conceded that the ascendancy also derived from a magical emanation from the man. He remembered from his days at Colgate an upperclassman who had the same mysterious ascendancy. For no particular reason this Clybairne occasionally appeared in Elligott's thoughts, and Elligott felt himself back down, as he had with Zuerner.

In consideration of his move to the Cape, where he could live the personality he chose, he resolved to contain himself so that nobody would ever again observe his limits in the sincerity of his smile, and have ascendancy over him.

Pleased by the exchange with Len, and enjoying the additional insight that he had risen a notch toward the status of old-timer, now that the heirs were gone, Elligott carried his newspaper the few steps to Dowling's.

As usual, others were there before him. He never managed
to be the coffee shop's first customer. Even when he arrived at
the opening minute and the door was unlocked for him, locals
were already there, having coffee; these were insiders, friends of
Dowling's who came through the kitchen door or grew in the
chairs, fungus.

Two of these insiders were at a table. He recognized them
and assumed they recognized him, although they were not ac-
quaintances, not even the order of acquaintance he would have
crossed a room in a distant city to greet as compatriots; at most he
might in, say, Milan have widened his eyes more generously and
nodded less curtly. They returned his signal in a way that indi-
cated they might not know him even in Nairobi.

Nobody was sitting at the counter, but someone had cluttered
what Elligott thought of as his regular place, at the kitchen end,
with a half-finished cup of milky coffee and a cigarette burning in
an ashtray. They would belong to a waitress. He disliked having to
choose a stool in unfamiliar territory. He felt exposed, diminished
in well-being. He was happy, however, to see that the doughnut
tray had arrived from the bakery and he would not have to eat
one of Dowling's double-sweet bran muffins. Brewed coffee
dripped into the Silex. On the stool he arranged the *Times* in the
order he would get to it: sports, business, front news, the rest.

Small tremors of alienation continued to assail him. He was
still not entirely used to having breakfast in a coffee shop. Men of
his rank had breakfast at home. Unless they were traveling, or
early meetings required them, they never entered restaurants, let
alone coffee shops, before lunch. It seemed illicit, a step over the
threshold to hell, a date with Sistie Evans. It took some getting
used to that among carpenters, telephone repairers, real-estate
agents, and insurance men were authentic businessmen, retired
like himself. They, too, had discovered late in life the pleasure of
coffee and a bakery doughnut that was neither staling nor slippery, not one of those mouse-skinned packaged doughnuts.

Where was the waitress?

With the Gabberts last night the subject of best-remembered meals had come up, which led to choices of what you would order if you were on Death Row. When his turn came, he said coffee and fresh cinnamon doughnuts.

They wouldn't accept a frivolous answer. He withdrew it. He asked Daisy to refresh him on what had been served that night at the governor's, still believing in the doughnuts and knowing in his soul that he mentioned dinner at the governor's only to tell the Gabberts he had been to such an event. Daisy did not remember the frogs' legs as all that remarkable.

A profile appeared in the window of the kitchen door, like a character on TV. A new blonde pushed in, not the dark girl with a dancer's tendony legs whom Elligott had expected.

While she hesitated, considering whether her first duty was to her coffee and burning cigarette or to the customer, he read her marked-down face and slightly funhouse-mirror figure, the fullnesses to be made marvelously compact throughout her life by tights, belts, bras, girdles, pantyhose, and the shiny, sanctifying nurse's uniform Dowling provided for his staff. She would smell like an hour in a motel.

"Coffee?"

"Black. Is there a cinnamon doughnut in that tray?"

She assembled the order, remembering at the last moment what Dowling had told her about picking up pastry with a waxed square. She filled the cup two-thirds full, placed the spoon with the bowl toward him. The tag read *Linda,* in Mrs. Dowling's childish cursive. The blonde reached for two cream cups and showed a tunnel between her breasts. Sexuality is whatever implies more. Elligott drifted forward to fall within her odor, but couldn't find it. Without drawing back from the counter she tilted her head to him, intimately; the gesture may have been something she picked up from her mother.

"Will that be all?"

Their eyes met precisely. She was no longer furniture of the establishment; she had come forward and was isolated with him.

"For now."

She closed her order book, stuffed it in the apron pocket, and walked away, around the end of the counter to take up again her cigarette and milky coffee. He felt that he had opened a conversation and had been rejected. When they picked up again, he would not be so subtle. He could ask her where she came from, what she did before, what schedule she worked.

He scanned the newspaper with an inattention that would have enraged the editor. He found nothing about why Pitt hadn't scored with all that first-half possession he had caught a mention of on the ten-o'clock news, only junk that came in before the paper went to bed: the weather and highlights from the first few series of downs, and nothing on Colgate other than the losing score. Unimportant golf and tennis this week. Horses. He didn't know anybody who paid attention to horses beyond the Derby-to-Belmont sequence in the spring, and the steeplechase, on account of Rolling Rock and Dick Mellon. Hockey was Catholic, a real Massachusetts sport for you. Basketball was black. Nobody he knew followed those sports until the playoffs. From yesterday's paper he already knew what his stocks had done. He scanned the section all the way back to the engineering jobs and didn't see anything about Interways making a new offer for Elligott Barge. He could see her in the back-counter mirror, poking at the falling-apart bundle of her hair.

He shifted the paper and looked around column one into the tunnel of her armpit. The girl was seamed with tunnels. Her raised arms drew her back erect, giving an inviting thrust to her figure. He mused that women could come off while looking you in the eye and combing their hair, while talking about flowers, money, baked potatoes, anything, just squeezing; the hidden agenda of mothers who told their little girls to keep their legs crossed. He willed the girl onto his wavelength: right guard not that many years ago at Colgate. A girl with a figure like hers wouldn't mind a little mature fattening. He watched for a sign, an eye flicker, that she was heating with him, but she finished with her hair and slumped into her mass. She seemed to have no spine. She subsided into wasted time, dribbling smoke.

He folded with a motion that caught her eye. He raised a hand to bring her to him to fill his cup, to try again to fall within her odor of cheap powder or sweat, it made no difference, and to tell her that all he wanted was an hour of the thousands she had to give carelessly away. Why should he have to look for a new way to say God's first truth? In the Beginning was no more or less than this moment. It wasn't as though he had nothing to bring to the transaction; he would give more than he asked—more want, more skill, more risk. Elligott, husband, father, grandfather, retired vice president of corporate relations, elder, member of duty boards. More risk.

He thought of her going back to the kitchen and asking Dowling what kind of creeps he had for customers. Linda and Dowling talking about him and laughing while they challenged each other in the narrow aisle in front of the work table. He couldn't find her odor. He imagined it from Sistie Evans forty-one years ago.

"I'll take a check."

She put it in front of him and wished him a nice day. He nodded briefly, as Zuerner would have. He put the paper together again, left her a quarter more than the usual change from the dollar so that she would remember him. Who was he? What did he do?

Walking out, he saw that the plumber Pauley had joined the two at the table. That reminded him to go home again by WAY TO THE DUMP. The girl ceased to exist for him.

Car key poised at the lock, he was suddenly disoriented. *How did I get here? Where am I going? Am I stopping, or about to start? Everything is too quiet for the amount of light.* As if it were an hour ago, people weren't coming and going to get the day moving. The purity of the air and the stillness were like the moment before a tornado; everyone had taken shelter. But, of course, it was Sunday, the hours were displaced. He started up and drove out of the lot.

Having grown up in the city, where nature was the lawn, the hedge, and the golf course, he had been slow to accept the grosser performances of nature, the turning seasons and rotation of flowers. Now he saw the texture of light, predicted weather from sunsets and fuzzy moons, identified the velvet red on the roadside as poison ivy, and leaves speckled like worm-infested apples as shrub cherries. He supposed he should have gone into the landscape-gardening business early.

Like two daring girls back just in time from an all-night party, an apricot maple and a maple more golden stood in the respectable green row that shaded the Pilgrim School. He rolled the window down far enough to get a better look at them, and then at the Betty Prior roses, the ones with a pale splash, piled along the fences. A great rose, out early and still holding; next spring he would put in a couple.

At Pauley's he slowed as he had when coming to town. He was driving so slowly that he might as well stop a moment and really look at the rhododendrons. He pulled onto the shoulder, dropped the keys on the floor, as was his habit, and went over.

Every finger of leaf had the thick look of health: none were browned or curled in distress. Buds were packed so tightly that they seemed ready to explode before wintering. But they would hold until spring, when great holiday bursts would show on the big broad-leafed plants, and the crisp varieties with small clustered leaves would light up like Christmas trees. No real rain had fallen since early July—where did they get their well-being? Pauley seemed unlikely to water stock this fat.

Elligott bent to the ground and scratched with a forefinger. Sandy black stuff, hard and dry as his own dirt. Did the old bog leach up here to wet the roots? Elligott didn't have a bog, but he had a hose, and the town water bill didn't amount to much. He looked for the angle of the sun and saw that it got in there a few hours every day, over the oaks, beyond where the wagon was stopped. His plantings at the Association got that much sun.

He noticed young plants a foot or two high scattered through the hedge. Probably grown from cuttings to replace the older stock. Maybe layered off the big stock. He felt for a branch that might loop into the ground and come up as a new plant. He found no connections, and decided the young plants must be cuttings.

Bent and reaching, Elligott now had an idea whose enormity tightened his chest. He pivoted to look both ways along the road. Carefully he opened the hedge to see the house. The shades were down.

Pauley owed him something for the time he had wasted waiting for the shower. Elligott grasped a plant by the throat and felt it break free of the top crust so easily that he reached for another and slung it under his arm. He looked again both ways on the road and quickly crossed.

Unlatching the tailgate delicately, to avoid a loud click, he laid the plants on the carpet. He was going around to the driver's door at the accelerated pace of someone not wanting to look pushy but nevertheless determined to get to the head of the line when he sensed an action at the house—a door or window opening—and somebody hollered, "What the hell are you doing there?"

Pauley's son.

He jumped into the seat while the voice pursued him; he dragged the door closed, found the key ring on the floor, stabbed at the ignition. The lock rejected the upside down key. He tumbled it home, jerk-started and stalled, and rammed his foot on the pedal to clear the flooded carburetor, thinking *Calm! Calm! Breathe!,* terrified that he had done himself in. He fought the key, and the engine caught at the moment frost sprang on the window lip, and he was struck on the side of the neck by what he experienced as hard-thrown gravel. He ducked and fell away from the blow and straightened again to control the careening wagon. *Get away from here fast!*

In seconds he was over a low rise and curve that distanced him from Pauley's place. He realized he was locked at mach 2, rigid arms and legs shoving him hard against the seat back. He relaxed a turn and took in air. As the tension eased from his shoulders and back, he became aware that his neck ached.

He put his hand to it and it came away wet. Blood. Blood

thin as water defined the creases and whorls of his palm. He was not prepared for blood. So much.

He wiped his hand on his new sweater and felt the wound with his fingertips. It felt like no more than an open boil, but the amount of blood scared him. He rolled his head to feel if the injury went deep. It seemed to stop at the surface. A spread of light shot? Had the man been lunatic enough to shoot because someone was poking in his bushes? What if the target had been some poor bastard with bad kidneys?

Christ, look at the blood! He eased the speed and held the wheel with his bloody hand while he reached around with the other for a handkerchief, but he hadn't put one in his pocket that morning. With his knees he held the wagon in line, though falling toward the berm, unbuttoned his sweater, and ripped open his shirt to get enough cloth to plaster against the wound. He hunched his neck to cramp the cloth tight. His mind set changed from *Get away!* to *Where to?* and he couldn't deal with the options.

Home was four minutes away, the hospital emergency branch was twelve by the shortcut back past Pauley's, but he couldn't even think of going back that way. The other road around the rotary was long, very long, and he was so very bloody, his neck cramped awkwardly against his shoulder. He tried to remember the name of the doctor who had a shingle at the lane going off after the next right, and what kind of doctor he was—or should he try for a paramedic on rescue-squad duty at the firehouse? He would have to do so much explaining. Had the wagon been identified? Just an old Chevy wagon. Who would believe it was his? His head felt enlarged, packed with engine noise and a mossy texture that resisted intelligence. It was only partly from the blow: his mind blurred in a crisis; he was not at his best at such times, he knew it, and there had never been a time quite like this.

The corner came at him faster than he could steady himself for it. The wagon waited for direction until the last instant before lunging over-steered toward the doctor, the Association, and home

almost out of habit—his hands grabbing for control of the slippery wheel. The wagon bolted across the eroded center line; the
tires washboarded, skidded, and sprayed berm. His neck jarred
loose from the bandage. He got back in lane while blood poured
down from the shoulder and sleeve of his sweater as if pumped.

As if pumped! It was more than he could get his mind
around. He had just gotten up and gone for a cup of coffee and a
doughnut, and his blood was slopping out down his arm into his
lap. He stuffed the wad of makeshift bandage back in place and
pressed hard against the wound; this is what you were supposed
to do to an artery wound—press hard, and not too long, or you
would black out. An *artery?* He refused the word, absorbed it into
the moss of his head.

Dr. Albert F. Bernhardt's sign came out of the brush like a
cue card to remind him that Daisy, joking, had said a psychiatrist
lived there, if they ever needed one. He raced past the psychiatrist
who wouldn't know anything about blood, about *arteries,* not as
much as an Eagle Scout, in a wagon full of blood and stolen
plants, and Zuerner on the way. A scrim of weakness fell. He
wanted to let his eyes close. He sobbed to suppress the percep-
tion that he could be dying and didn't know what to do about
Zuerner's coming just in time to find out that he stole plants in
the neighborhood.

A small gray car, the first traffic on the road that morning,
closed toward him, and he roused to the thought of something
better than sleep: obliteration. A smashup jumbling and conceal-
ing everything, everything wiped out, blood explained in bashed
rolling metal and fire.

The small car came on as innocent of danger and terror as
he himself had been a short while ago. Catholics going to church.
It would be easy, fast, over.

At the moment, the only moment he had, he was incapable
of aiming. He felt a blurt of nobility as the small gray car went by.
Did they see the blood? Did they think he held his head this way
because he was sleepy? Did they know he held their lives in his

hand for a moment and was merciful? He was a merciful man with no possession in the world but mercy, and to strangers, and nobody was there to sign his card.

The wagon was at the fork where the Association road came in. Barely driven, it was taking him home to tell Daisy to protect him from Zuerner. Daisy would clean up everything and think of a plausible story. He found the least strength necessary to guide onto the sudden rough and sounding surface.

He couldn't bother to steer around potholes. He went down the crown of the dirt road, jouncing and pounding the shocks, slack hand on the wheel like a dozing passenger. At the turnoff to his own driveway he knew he wasn't going to get to Daisy. He was gone, he didn't have time to tell Daisy what she had to do. He was going to pass out. In a gravel-scattering skid he entered his own long, curving drive at forty, forty-five, fifty, toward the open garage door that waited to swallow him against the far wall and create a mystery (heart attack? pedal stuck?), his name intact.

Elligott now had his last great idea of the morning.

Alongside the garage the land sloped to the cove through an insubstantial hedge of nursery plants—forsythia, hydrangea, cinquefoil, and the like—and, lower down, wild honeysuckle, briar, and saplings that had volunteered to try again where the city people had cleared. At the foot the returning tide infiltrated the bordering marsh grass.

The possibility came to him almost too late to act on. With nothing measurable to spare he veered past the corner of the garage and over the sunk railroad tie that defined the hedge line, trashed the honeysuckle, flailed through a berserk car wash of saplings, briar, rugosas, grapevines, forcing all the momentum he could into the wagon to scar through the soft wetland and on into the cove where the thrust ended almost gently, like a boat with a sail dropped or an engine cut.

The wagon tilted on a rock and stopped.

He would have to stay in motion to keep from blacking out. He pulled the latch; his weight pushed the door open and he slumped with it clumsily into a tide that took him at the knee. By noon it would be chest-high. He steadied on the door. Everything was quiet after the last tearing minutes. *Forget the plants. Can't lift the door. Not unusual to carry plants in the wagon. Water will make a slop back there, mix everything up. Keep moving.*

He staggered around the drowning wagon, slipping on bottom rocks greasy with eelgrass. He glanced up at his house. Through sagging eyelids he saw that it was handsome in the early sun. He started to take his hand from the bloody bundle at his neck so he could look at his watch and verify the time, but he knew at once that the gesture was too foolish to complete. If only Daisy would appear, they could wave good-bye to each other.

Crouched, balancing with his free arm like a remembered sepia picture of a farmer scattering grain, he lurched against the heavy purpose of the tide, toward no vision of a further life or of beings natural or supernatural intended to be called up by ten thousand Sunday-morning mumblings. That and all love, error, and regret; all papers on his desk, all letters, all unkempt plantings, all things unsaid to Daisy and Margie and the grandchildren and the judge in the traffic court: gone, irretrievable. His last mercy dispensed. His last desire a girl in a doughnut shop. His last act theft. Only honor was now left to him.

His new sweater sucked up a weight of water. He swayed and stumbled over the unstable bottom. His eyes closed to a minimum blur of light and form. His head hung forward. The hand that held the blood-wet cloth failed to his side. He dragged one more step, and another, and another toward the obscure channel hidden in the grass over there where an hour ago he had imagined sneaking the net under big blue crabs so that Zuerner would sign his card. Elligott, a man whose name had decided his work and chosen his wife; and she had brought him to this place where a stranger with a gun decided when he was to die.

Or was it Zuerner, who would follow him everywhere, who had decided? Caving to his knees, fainting, falling toward drowning, his impression (the vapor of exhaustion could no longer be called something as coherent as thought)—his impression was that to die this worthily was an act of transcendent honor; beyond the comprehension of a man like Zuerner. And yet, the vapor formed, faded; what is Zuerner to me that I give him my life?

Notes

E. S. Goldman didn't know for sure what "Way to the Dump" was about when he began writing. "The last sentence is what the story is about, *and I didn't find it out until I had got to the end and heard myself saying it.* I knew I would find the exact end if I just got into the area with the succession of incidents and descriptions I had jotted on a piece of paper when I began to write. After discovering the end I had to backtrack through the story and heighten the clues."

It may seem strange that a writer would begin a story with little idea where it's going. But Goldman's editor, *Atlantic Monthly* senior editor C. Michael Curtis, isn't surprised. "That's a familiar enough position, and a lot of writers will say that," he says. "I know it's sometimes a bit puzzling because you look at the work and it seems to be integrated and to follow some sort of internal logic. My best guess is that the writer isn't always aware of that internal logic. That the story at some point begins to take on a life of its own and it simply flows."

Curtis says that discovering the story as you write is not only common, but sometimes an advantage. "In many cases, that's the kind of story readers respond to more than a story that is studied and calculated, that seems to readers to be more contrived and artificial."

That kind of gut-level reaction is what Curtis and the other editors at the *Atlantic* look for as they sort through the 12,000 stories a year they receive. "When one comes through that seems to us to have the elements of story, and to be written in a way that is convincing and moving and coherent and, ideally, original, we simply respond. We don't respond as literary critics, we respond on some visceral level in the sense that reading these stories has produced a kind of instantaneous and authentic response that we think is valuable."

While Goldman says he didn't discover his ending until he got there, the issue it deals with—whether a person should rely on others' opinions or trust his or her own judgment—has long been important to him. He says the story "is about a man who for no good reason places himself in a psychologically inferior position to another man, and destroys himself. In the end, too late, he has a glimmer of what he has done."

That's a pitfall Goldman has always tried to avoid. For most of his life, he has written for himself and not to get published. Other than one story published by the pulp magazine *Adventure* in 1944 (which I decided was long enough ago and minor enough that it didn't disqualify Goldman from inclusion here), he had no career in fiction until he was seventy-five. Then Curtis bought a story called "Dog People" and, shortly afterward, "Way to the Dump," which was published first. The same year his novel *Big Chocolate Cookies* was accepted by John Daniel, Publisher.

"What can you possibly learn from that?" Goldman asks. "That if you write fiction all your life for the sheer pleasure of writing, in exactly the way you want to write—just as you might be a Sunday painter or an opera buff with strict standards but without contemplating a professional career in art or music—then in your seventy-fifth year, after you have retired from business, by a series of accidents you may earn an extremely modest income from fiction."

His determination to write for the joy of it is evident in his response to the news that Curtis had accepted his story. He was writing when Curtis called and calmly finished what he was doing before going to tell his wife the good news. "Don't misunderstand me," he says. "I like to be published, but it cannot compare with the elation that comes from getting the writing right in my own judgment."

Getting it right requires lots of rewriting. Goldman sits at the word processor—which he says is exactly suited to his writing habits—at least five hours a day, six or seven days a week. "I do not believe in writer's block," he says. "Some sentences are written, moved elsewhere, and generally fiddled with twenty times. As far as I am concerned a story is never finished."

It's never easy, either. When asked what aspect of writing he finds most difficult, he says, "It's hardest to get the first paragraph right. Then the last paragraph. Then the fifth paragraph. The whole damn thing is hard."

Goldman says "Way to the Dump" had no "flash-of-light" inspiration. "It is one of many whose germinal idea seemed good enough to jot down with a few notes some years ago." When he's ready to work on a new story Goldman goes through the file to "see if any of those ideas wants to talk to me today."

Little of his fiction is based on reality. "I seldom write a story with characters from life (except incidental people). Fragments of experienced personality and incidents are drawn into the stream of writing once it begins." The exception is setting. "I don't see much purpose in inventing geography. It's there for the taking, to distort enough for the need."

He also doesn't choose a point of view. "Before a story feels ready to be written I hear it in the voice that will tell it. The novel *Big Chocolate Cookies,* for example, wouldn't have been written if I hadn't heard it in the narrator's peculiar voice."

Goldman sent "Way to the Dump" to three or four other magazines before the *Atlantic.* Curtis, having already bought "Dog People," accepted it within a week. Curtis sees the story as being "about someone who is unexpectedly undone by his history, by his failures and his fears over time, and the way those experiences lead him to blunder."

When he accepted the first story, Curtis had no idea that Goldman hadn't been published before. "I didn't know whether E. S. Goldman was a man or a woman or how old he was or anything about him," he says. "We responded simply to the quality of his work." Curtis says it's a misconception that only established writers are published in the *Atlantic.* "We do in fact read stories and publish stories by writers who have no prior connection here. . . . It's the kind of thing we most enjoy doing."

Curtis's revisions were minor, Goldman says—queries to his "quirky" vocabulary and changes required by the *Atlantic* stylebook. "Editors are extraordinarily good readers," Goldman says. "As long as the options remain mine, I hope they propose every change they think may be valid."

At the *Atlantic,* the option does remain with the author. "We don't do any editing unless we have the approval of the author and what that means in turn is that most writers are generally grateful for our efforts on their behalf," Curtis says.

Curtis is hesitant to request extensive changes to a story and, like Goldman, warns writers against doing too much to please an editor. "Our experience is that when a writer begins to tinker with a story that somehow it isn't really better and in many cases it's even worse. It's a treacherous exercise. I'm not even sure that I think writers ought to do it—that is, unless they're dead sure they want to make changes because they themselves see something wrong. I'm not at all sure they should try to write to satisfy an editor. It could be that they just ought to sell the story where they can sell it and send that editor another story."

That approach works for Goldman, at least. He's now sold six stories, including a third to Curtis, and his novel has gone into a second printing and earned a film option. "Way to the Dump" was published in *Best American Short Stories 1988*. He's written thirty stories altogether, and is circulating four of those. He's also finishing a second novel.

But he remains skeptical of outside opinion. "Another story, 'The Grande Open' is the best story I ever wrote or am likely to write and no editor has ever been the least interested in it," he points out.

So it's no surprise that this is his advice to other writers: "Enjoy writing for itself, not because it gets the approval of publication."

Little Saigon

for Warren Fine, 1943–1987

Between O Street and Vine, there's a six block stretch of 27th Street that has four oriental markets. They're mom-and-pop joints, with names like A Long, Vien Dao, Ayuttayah. The stores are practically closets with high teetering shelves and every kind of thing for sale: rice cakes, and postcards, dolls, fish paste, movie magazines, bee pollen, unguent, noodles and things that look too odd to think about.

Twenty-seventh cuts the poor part of town in two. To the west is the home for the afflicted and a lot of black people with their ribshack and barber shop. To the east are poor folks of all kinds: college students, white women with brown babies, more blacks, old people, Vietnamese, Cambodians and a darker race I can't name.

There's no municipal collection in this town, everybody has to contract with a private service or take it to the dump themselves. It's wonderful what people throw away. One afternoon I watched a kid and his older sister throw hundreds of stereo records out of the back of an old green pickup, skimming them like frisbees at the gulls screaming over the dump.

Another time the neighbor woman told me as a joke to bring her home a lamp, so I asked her what color. "How about yellow?" she said. And I brought her home a yellow lamp. Her husband rewired it and they've got it in their livingroom yet.

We hit the alleys at dawn, the boss and a black man named Wardell and me. For the other side of the tracks it's a real nice neighborhood, good trees, a half dozen American elms that survived the plague years, big frame and brick houses built around the turn of the century up to the thirties until the Great Depres-

sion put shut to all that. I stood one day on the street counting
the kids on the porch of one high green house. I made out seventeen. A guy washing his Mustang by the curb looked at me over
his shades and laughed. "These only the least ones. The rest in
school."

The refugees live two and three families to the house, or else
they have a different idea of family: many children, the women old
and young in their long skirts and headscarves and straw hats, lots
of teenagers. I notice there aren't too many middle-aged men. The
young ones all have cars, beat up Chevs and Buicks around fifteen
years old, or at least bicycles. In warm weather you can hear the
top forty they love and Vietnamese music too in a spooky mix.

Then about every block has a few old couples, maybe a
widow or a couple divorcees, holdovers from the forties and before. They set their garbage in little brick pens against the dogs.
Their yards are as clean as stovetops.

One morning in early summer one of these older ladies
stopped the boss to tell him something. He left the truck idling in
the alley. Wardell and I were throwing plastic sacks in the back.
She wanted to know if we'd seen her dog, a brown setter.

"No Ma'am," said the boss, fingering his seedcap.

"It's these boat people," she told us. She had on an old blue
wrapper and a net over her little rag of blue hair. "It's just not like
Lady to worry me. Mrs. Pavelka's dog disappeared last month. It's
those teenage boys, I think they steal them, and they sell them."

"Gee," said the boss who looks like Gary Cooper if he'd
been through a real war, done all his own stunt work and lived to
be an old plug who still didn't have two words to say. He's lived
all his life in the one town, veteran of Korea, pays cash, good man
to work for but not much for meeting the public.

"Don't worry, ma'am," he said sincerely. "I'm sure your dog
will come home."

I swung up on the back of the truck with Wardell. "They
probably done eat it," he said.

"Gimme a break."

"I'm serious," said Wardell. "In the orient, dog is a delicacy."
He smiled.

The boss escaped from the old lady and got in the cab,
popped the clutch and we lurched away.

"In China," yelled Wardell, clinging to the tailgate as we
jounced down the alley, eating our own dust, "rich men eat dog
on their birthday."

Lots of people in this town make gardens: sweet corn, cukes,
zucchini, plenty of tomatoes. But these Vietnamese gardens are way
out of their league. The old women are garden geniuses, they don't
waste a thing. Every scrap goes back on for compost, and the beds
are shored up with brick and cement block and boards they pull
down from old garages in the alley. They grow roots with lacy tops,
kneedeep greens, eggplant, many kinds of squashes and peas,
yams, flowering things and herbs, everything growing jammed up,
not an inch for a weed to show its ugly head, all watered by hand-
carried can, thriving like somebody's life depended on it.

Right in the middle of one garden, one of these old refugee
ladies built a shrine. That is, she supervised the bunch of teenage
boys who did the work. For days they were pouring concrete and
laying brick, jeans rolled up and slipping off their skinny hips. The
base was about three feet high and it had a lot of Vietnamese
words on it spelled out in the kind of letters people use on mailboxes. At first we thought it might be a base for a satellite dish.
But when it was done, there was a white plaster Jesus standing up
to the morning sun, bright red heart clasped to his breast in his
white hands.

One day Wardell said to me, "I guess it was a lot of Catholics
in Vietnam on account of the French. You think?"

"Could be," I said. "Never thought about it."

"Kennedy was a Catholic. How come he never went to
Nam like L B J did? Didn't want to call no attention to the family
resemblance?"

"The mafia are Catholics too. So what? And the conquistado-
res. Catholics are everywhere."

"I'm not talking about the mafia," he said. "It's just, you know, a curiosity. All those monks barbecuing themselves, you remember? I keep thinking about that mama-san or somebody praying—let me over that embassy wall, Lord Jesus don't let the boat sink. Please take me on dry land, Captain, and whenever I get my ass to the US of A, I swear I'll put you up a totem pole, Sweet Jesus Savior of my soul."

About a week later, the dog lady met us by her garage with a couple of policemen. She'd had them investigating the cans in her alley, and now she wanted them to search our truck.

The boss protested. "I give you my word I got nothing in there but trash. I told you I'd tell you if we saw your dog."

She was all puffed up with grief and civic outrage. "Mrs. Sloan's cat has been gone since Thursday night," she said. "I want to get to the bottom of this."

"You want us to comb through all that?" Wardell spit.

The boss appealed to the cops. "I got a schedule," he said. "People don't like to look at their trash, that's why they pay me."

But cops can't just ignore a complaint. That's what they're paid for, and anyway, it's not in their temperament.

"It ain't in my contract," said Wardell, moving away from the truck. He jerked his chin at me. "His either. No way."

We don't have any contract, but we went and stood over by somebody else's garage while the boss and the cops dragged sacks out of the truck and opened them. Then the boss put on his waders and climbed in with the loose stuff, poking around while the cops stuck their heads over the side.

"What a Tom," said Wardell.

"He's not even black, Wardell."

"Which makes him a chucklehead as well as a Tom."

The cops were nearly gagging. They didn't find anything: just paper, cans, rotten food and shitty diapers, broken glass, different kinds of dusty crud and slime. The regular stuff.

Dogs are always after the cans, rolling them over to get the lids off. One morning we came on a German shepherd gnawing at a chunk of meat in a brown paper sack.

"Get outta here, dogshit," said Wardell, kicking him away. I bent down to pick up the sack and saw what it was.

"Whoa to Jesus," said Wardell.

It was the head of a dog, skinned out and pretty old. It still had eyes, but the ears were gone and you couldn't really tell what breed it was. Wardell yelled for the boss.

"God dawg," he said, hanging in his blue jeans there like a tree that can't decide which way to fall. Then he took Wardell's shovel and flipped the head into the truck. He looked at me, then Wardell, like he was daring us to twitch.

"That wasn't her dog," he said.

"No sir," I said.

A Vietnamese kid, little girl in a skimpy dress and cowboy boots stood over by a clothesline, watching us with her eyes like cups of black tea.

The boss got in the cab and slammed the door. He called out the window. "And cover it up quick."

I did and then grabbed on for my dear life as the boss jammed into reverse and backed wildly down the alley, bell ringing like a frantic leper.

The dog lady kept stopping us to tell us to watch for animal remains. She was keeping a census of all the disappeared pets. She made some signs with Lady's picture and tacked them on phone poles over the ads for garage sales. Soon the old people on her block were all keeping their cats and dogs indoors, and the metermen and delivery boys were taking the long way around to keep from meeting her, nervous as nits.

We caught her poking in her neighbors' cans. The Vietnamese don't throw away too much, a little paper, a few jars. You can tell a lot about people by what they throw away. It's just another kind of archaeology.

Then one morning we pulled into the alley with a black-and-white right behind us. The dog lady was hovering over her own garbage can. She was wild. "Look!" she yelled. "You men look here!"

The can was filled with parts of dogs, legs and heads mostly, some partly frozen. There was a headless half, ribs and shoulders, plenty of meat but gone off, I guess. The joker responsible had included a whole possum, roadkill and extra high.

"Proof?" she said. "You want proof? Here it is. Scientific proof."

We helped the cops check out all the other cans in the alley. They didn't seem anxious to start knocking at random on the backdoors. Nobody was even out that morning: no kids, no dogs, no mama-sans, just the blinded windows of the houses and Jesus in his garden with his heart in his hands. The sky was one smeary cloud and a lot of wind, threatening rain.

The boss offered to take the dog parts away, but the cops said they had to take them in to make their report. The dog lady gave one cop her statement in her loud old vinegar voice while Wardell held the bag and I forked the evidence in.

"You want the possum, too?" I asked the other cop, all spit, polish and stiff blue shirt, who was kind of gauging us out of the corner of his eye.

"It's all evidence."

"Man," Wardell said to no one, tying off the bags. "I would not have his job."

The boss took us to breakfast. He was a long time washing his hands, then came and sat down in the booth by Wardell. He took off his seedcap and scratched his big head.

"Well and I don't know what to think about those people," he said at last. "You guys think they really eat them dogs?"

"Indians up on the reservation eat dog, or they used to," I said. "They eat dog in Africa, Wardell?"

"Your mouth, whitefolks," he said. He lit a cigarette and sighted down its length at me. "I don't mean to sound like a bigot, but what do you think a bunch of refugees care about a pack of stinking dogs?"

"This ain't Vietnam," said the boss. "These dogs are pets. Some of these old folks, their dog is all they got. You can't eat people's pets, for Chrissake."

"Lemme tell you something," said Wardell. "These folks have cockroaches for pets. They be having motherfucking rats for they pets. And they won't always be eating your dogs, either. The kids grow up watching TV, be going to your schools. Pretty soon they start to think eating dog's not cool, they learn how to be American, act just like you and me."

The cafe windows faced 27th. Outside, the broad street intersected the railroad tracks then ran south towards O Street lined with thriftstores, laundromats, one-story and everything the color of dust under the uncertain sky. A man on a bike bumped over the tracks, a woman in a long skirt pulling a child in a wagon stooped to look into a store window, a pickup with muddy fenders and crates of live chickens in back rolled by. Inside, it was cool and the boss leaned his head against the window.

"I don't understand," he said.

"Hey," said Wardell. "In a few years these refugees be sorry. They will be sorry they ate your dogs. It's just, you know, sorry take time. We sorry NOW about all that napalm. Folks sorry NOW Martin and Bobby and them got killed. These folks going to be sorry too, man, and sorry take time."

Notes

"Little Saigon" has—I almost hesitate to say it—a point. I wouldn't go so far as to call it a moral, but Sally Herrin definitely has something to say in this story.

She explains it like this: "Lasting change takes a long, long time. I really wanted that truth to be in there. But at the same time, I really like to put incompatible truths in the mouths of people. I'm serious when I have the boss say, 'You can't eat people's pets. Some of these old people, their pets are all they have.' And that's right—you can't eat people's pets. On the other hand, it's also true that people from another society, in their eyes a particular animal may not have the kind of emotional sanctity that a pet would have for us."

Those "incompatible truths" intrigued Bob Shar, former editor of the *Crescent Review*. He liked the way Herrin contrasted the Vietnamese refugees' actions with those of American society. "The atrocities we're now sorry about—we're sorry about the napalm and we're sorry about the blacks that got lynched—set up against the fact that these people *ate a dog*. The comparison is staggering. It says something about the way we see the world, how people can get so morally outraged about things that in the long run are absurd, and go along with the crowd about things that truly are outrageous."

Even though stories that have a point to make seem to be out of fashion in some literary circles, Shar likes them. "It depends on how it's executed—you don't want to be bludgeoned over the head with the moral—but if you're going to spend time reading a story, I feel like you should come away a little richer. You ought to have something to think about—the story ought to go on beyond the page."

But while both Herrin and Shar think the fact that "Little Saigon" is somewhat political is one of its strengths, they both worried over one aspect: Could the story be construed as racist? One magazine rejected the story on those grounds.

"I only worried about that briefly, because from my point of view it's not racist at all," Herrin says. "In fact, it's anti-racist." She says the story tries to promote racial understanding by showing how a particular action, in this case eating dogs, might look from a different perspective—without being too obvious about it. "I try to let racism comment on itself, rather than make any pointed comment about racism in my text. When Wardell says, 'These people have cockroaches for pets' that's about as didactic as I get."

"It did concern me," Shar says. "In terms of how a Vietnamese reader might feel, again thinking beyond the printed page, it was unsettling."

But Shar felt that Wardell's closing comments would put to rest any concerns about racism, and decided to publish it.

That decision was the culmination of a long birthing process for "Little Saigon." Herrin had written poetry for years, but didn't start writing fiction until 1983, just before she finished her doctorate in English at the University of Nebraska-Lincoln. That spring, her mother died. "I was trying to cheer myself up. That was really the beginning of my serious fiction writing, and I've been writing short stories since then," she says.

She had seven weeks between graduate school and her first teaching job, so she promised herself she'd write a story a week—and did. "Little Saigon" was the first of those stories.

The idea for the story came from life. Herrin lived in the Lincoln neighborhood where the story is set and one day found her dog, Jesse, playing with a paper bag. When she checked on it, Herrin found that the bag contained the head of a dog.

"I was just overwhelmed by it, and I had to do something to deal with it, so I wrote the story," Herrin says. "It was just too good to pass up for a writer, something like that happening."

But the story also had a deeper inspiration. Herrin's family lived in Thailand for a year when she was seven, and she feels a tie with Southeast Asia. Because of that, she was interested in how the refugees in her neighborhood fit in with the tradition of settlers who preceded them.

"I was intrigued with how they have continued the story that all Great Plains literature reflects," she says. "This part of the country has not been that hospitable to permanent settlement. The refugees are gradually becoming assimilated, and yet they'll always color this area too, in the same way that the other groups who've lived here have colored it. So that was sort of my subtext."

Herrin revised and rewrote the story three or four times over a period of two years, using her husband, Charles Flowerday, who is also a writer and editor, for a sounding board.

Most of the work was on the Wardell character. "He's not based on a person I know, so I had to come up with him. He had to really become alive inside me in some way."

Wardell was crucial because he serves as the moral center for the story, Herrin says. "That last statement where he says, 'Sorry takes time' really means a lot to me. I worked to make Wardell creditable enough that he could say that."

She says she made him black "because he had to be able to perceive the situation not in exactly mainstream terms." She wanted him to be "earthy and smart and, to some degree, politically thoughtful, but not a formally educated person."

She also spent a good deal of time on the dialogue, particularly Wardell's. She relied on her experience as a food stamp case worker in Atlanta to give his speech an authentic sound. In one version, she tried to use phonetic spelling, but it was awkward. She eliminated it after rereading Faulkner. "I found that he uses standard English spelling and somehow is able to convey Southern speech through the rhythms and through the diction."

After being rejected by about three magazines, Herrin noticed a listing in the *International Directory of Little Magazines and Small Presses* by Dustbooks. The listing said the *Crescent Review* was looking for "unpublished and underpublished Southeastern writers." Herrin, who went to high school in Atlanta, sent the story, along with a letter saying she was the very definition of that criterion.

Shar liked her slightly self-deprecating tone and her story. "I almost took it more for what it was *not* than for what it was, in that it was not a typical story—not about a struggling writer or a corrupt professor. An enormous amount of stories about writers were coming in at the time. It's the 'Henry James syndrome'—you're supposed to write about what you know, so people in MFA programs write about writing."

But it wasn't only what the story wasn't. "The narrator's voice seemed right, Wardell's seemed right," Shar says. "And I loved the description of the boss—the comparison to Gary Cooper is wonderful."

Shar requested few changes. "I had some very minor quibbles about voice," he says. "The narrator said a few words that seemed out of character." For instance, in the second paragraph the narrator said, "To the east are poor folks of all kinds: college students, white women with mulatto children, more blacks, old people, Vietnamese, Cambodians and a darker race I can't name." Shar suggested that Herrin change "mulatto children" to "brown babies."

Herrin liked that suggestion and accepted it, but she resisted another change. Shar recommended that she cut the paragraph where the narrator talks about getting a lamp from the dump for one of his neighbors. Herrin explained that she liked "the idea of light, illumination coming from garbage" and Shar agreed to leave the paragraph in place.

"I really feel like I connected with Bob Shar," Herrin says. "He had good instincts about the story. I wouldn't be willing to make just any compromise in order to get published, but you have to recognize the people who have good instincts about your work and not feel too threatened."

Herrin says there is only one aspect of the story she might change now. After "Little Saigon" was published, she read something that made her wonder if, contrary to what the story says, John F. Kennedy visited Vietnam. "If I had it to do over again, I'd research that and make sure," she says.

But overall she likes the story. "I think it's a funny story, and if I succeed as a writer it'll be because my stories are funny. I also think it is human somehow."

Private Lies

One.

The two places I have lived that do not count are these:

The apartment in Los Angeles where my father's company put us before our house was ready: a large, impersonal series of rooms, connected by archways rather than doors, with walls so textured my father was constantly scratching the crystal of his watch when he gestured.

My sister was nine and I was seven, and together with my father we lived in that apartment at first as if in quarantine, cautiously testing the brown air on those first few trips to the supermarket, getting used to heat without humidity, adjusting to the natives who met bad weather with suspicion and drove with their headlights on in the middle of the afternoon in the lightest drizzle.

I recall only two particulars of that summer: the transition from training wheels to a blue two-wheeler with a sparkle seat and the daily postcards from my mother, who was still in Philadelphia trying to sell the house before she joined us on the West Coast. The postcards were usually of historic sites or landmarks in Philadelphia, and over the course of the summer we received several of the same card. By August we counted eight postcards of the Liberty Bell between us. I remember this, I remember her absence.

Many years later, in a high-school botany course, I learned about plants that project energy out of limbs that have been severed, and I thought of the three of us that summer, and my mother miles and miles away.

Then there is my father's house, high up in the Hollywood Hills, where he lives with his wife and a large, foul-tempered dog named Derby. These days I visit infrequently: a long weekend every summer, but more often just for dinner when I am in town. On those occasions we have cocktails in the living room and everyone waits for me to mention the view, which then dominates the conversation. Actually, it is a spectacular view, the best thing about the house. My father walks with me out to the terrace and points out the lights of the city below that form their own strange constellations: the back lot of MGM, the airport runway, the revolving restaurant on top of the Hilton, where someone I once knew had a bridal shower and then neglected to go through with the wedding.

The house is hard to find, since all the houses in that area were built by the same developer and are difficult to tell apart, all of them variations on some A-frame theme. The street names are also too much the same. Testaments to some city planner's lack of imagination, they're all Oakridges or Elmwoods, Birchways or Pineboughs. Several times I have seen my father turn down the wrong street, and then swear and slam the car into reverse, embarrassed that I'm there in the car witnessing his mistake. He's lived there for over seven years.

I stopped keeping a set of directions to the house in my wallet the year my father stopped asking me how my mother was. The house in the hills does not count because a home is not a place you need directions to find. And, of course, there are other reasons.

Because I no longer keep a set of directions in my wallet, periodically I need to call my father from the Gulf station phone on the corner of Sunset Boulevard and the main turnoff. I call him and say that I am lost.

Two.

My mother ships me boxes of things she thinks I need in my new apartment: kitchen utensils, a bath mat, candlesticks, a lamp, dishes. In a way, I am doing her the favor; her own small apartment is filled with all of the things she kept from the Los Angeles house, either out of a professed fondness, or out of spite.

For weeks I let these boxes pile up in my hallway, until she phones, her voice thin and hurt, seeking an itemized acknowledgement. And so I open them, separating the breakables from the newspapers, untangling cords, stacking pots and dishes. There is no closet space here in this new place and I will be months finding a spot for everything.

These things are all familiar to me, though I haven't seen them for many years. I remember the bath mat that doubled as a magic carpet, the spanking inflicted for playing tag inside and chipping the serving plate. And looking at these things, that house is conjured.

It was a huge house, far too big for the four of us. My father, heady with his new board chairmanship, delighted in its scale: a foyer as big as the four-car garage, his and her bathrooms, an oak tree at the foot of the driveway the four of us couldn't wrap our arms around. For years he proudly announced to guests that there were several rooms they hadn't even bothered to furnish. My mother, at first overwhelmed by its opulence, came to call it her dream house. She spent months with decorators, choosing wallpaper and end tables, going from room to room with her fabric swatches, looking at the colors in different light.

Before us, the house had belonged to a second-rate film director, a man known in the business for his third wife, their splashy divorce and the amount of her monthly alimony. This former presence enthralled my sister and me for the better part of our adolescence and ignited our imaginations. We spent afternoons playing Screen Test, an empty director's chair before us, or staging Hollywood gatherings; I, in deference to my sister's age, playing the male escorts to her leading ladies.

Built before the Depression, the house felt old and solid. The ceilings were very high; the tile in the kitchen came from a Mexican palace; the plumbing always gave us trouble. Occasional earthquakes cracked plaster around the door frames, but that was all. The walls were made of concrete so thick you could never hear arguments, even if they were coming from the next room.

Despite its size, the house never felt too big, at least not until the very end, when my father moved into one of the spare bedrooms. And then that distance between my parents' rooms seemed twice the length of the house.

Where was I for the dividing up, the parceling out of property? At a friend's house? At summer camp? Upstairs, asleep? I imagined the two of them like Hollywood gangsters splitting the take: that for you, this for me, that for you, this for me. If there was dissension, I only learned of it much later when my father would ask about something; he'd ask, for instance, had my mother hung the painting in good light? I saw, also, my mother's small smile when she learned that my father broke his collarbone tripping on the welcome mat they had bought one summer in Mexico.

There was the day I came home to find everything tagged blue or red so the moving men would know in which truck things belonged. Neither my mother nor my father had wanted the living-room rug, so it was the one thing left behind. Dimpled with markings of the furniture legs, darkened with cigarette ash near where the coffee table had been and splotched red from my illicit experiments with sealing wax, it told too clearly of a family that had, for seven years, lived on its surface.

The house seemed almost small when we left, as if the walls had contracted with our leaving.

Three.

There were some things I was aware of even then.

The telephone rang too often during dinner for there not to have been many affairs in my family. We would be seated at the table and the phone would ring once, twice, and then my mother would say in too resigned a tone, "I'll get it," even though none of us had made a motion to stand. She'd push through the swinging doors that led to the kitchen, and as they fluttered for a moment before clapping shut, we'd hear her answer, "Hello," and then, deeper, quieter, a second "Hello," sometimes a soft laugh.

My father, who rarely spoke at meals, chose these times to ask us about school, to ask about a best friend, to ask who was riding in the car pool these days and did Daphne's parents ever intend to fix that overbite of hers? My sister and I would fabricate long, involved responses, which we delivered in loud, very loud, voices. School was okay, but the report on Eskimos had gotten a B, even *with* the igloo diorama, and everyone thought Mrs. Delano was half-woman, half-man because she kind of had a mustache and her pants bagged funny.

My mother's conversations were never long. She would return to the table, smooth her napkin on her lap in short, punctuated gestures and offer brief explanations. "Irene," she'd say with irritation. "I wish she'd remember not to call at dinnertime," as if the oversight alone was sufficient reason for the call. The explanations were never more involved than that: a name, a survey, a dinner invitation, a wrong number.

She told us that the smog was too much for her and that she'd have to drive down the coast for a few days for her lungs to clear.

She told us the phone was out of order the afternoon the school bus had a flat and we had tried to call her for an hour and a half from the pay phone in the attendance office.

She told us she fired the maid because the woman just could not learn to make a bed correctly.

She told us the cardigan was left by the pool man.

We looked away, said nothing, when she said these things. For years, I thought our silence made us conspirators, accomplices to her infidelity.

Four.

Even years later, we did not speak of these things, or cite them as reasons for the divorce.

They married too young. It was time for them to grow up.

They grew in different directions.

They grew apart.

Growth was the explanation we gave to relatives, friends and lovers... offered to psychiatrists, as if marriages were arrangements made in weakness or out of carelessness, and separation was somehow synonymous with maturity.

Once, my sister drove in to meet me at O'Hare, where my flight to Boston had a two-hour layover. We sat in the airport bar, looking out at the runway as the planes taxied in and out. I folded my cocktail napkin into a tiny square as we joked about the sameness of airport bars: the heavy decor, the wood paneling, the predictability of their names, always Drummond's or Greenhill's.

She talked about the work she was doing, restoration at the Art Institute, and of the man she was involved with who was putting himself through night school by installing traffic lights during the day. She'd started therapy again, she said, to work out some of her dreams, and then, suddenly, she asked, Did I know any of the men Mother had slept with?

In the pause, I lighted a cigarette and she flagged the bartender for another drink. We both let the question pass as an aside, as if it had been an exercise in word association: therapy, dreams, affairs. I excused myself to go to the restroom, where I stood for a long time outside the only stall, until a young girl, 16 or 17, emerged, and said to me, apologetically, that she'd had trouble putting in her diaphragm.

At the time, my mind dulled by two vodkas, I did not think it strange for a young girl to be inserting her diaphragm in the bathroom of an airport bar, only an unusual admission to make to me, a complete stranger. Later, memory connected these two incidents by something more than their concurrence or locale: my sister, whom I had not seen for many months, drinking daiquiris, telling me she was letting her hair grow long, asking me about our mother's lovers; this young girl in jeans, cowboy boots and a ski parka, apologizing and explaining her delay. It wasn't an outraged sense of propriety or a bruised naïveté that connected the two and, in

retrospect, disturbed me the most. Rather, it was a deep resent-
ment at being made a confidant, a witness to situations with im-
plications I did not want to know.

My sister and I did not say much to each other for the rest
of our time together. I had another drink because I don't like to
fly, and we argued over the check, which she paid. It was announced that my flight was boarding, and we walked arm and
arm to the gate.

We said that we'd see each other soon, that fares would be
going down in a few months, or maybe she'd drive out with the
traffic-light installer when the weather got better.

Then I told her that, no, I hadn't known any of the men our
mother had slept with, I had never wanted to know who they
were. We hugged each other for a long time and I boarded the
plane and flew to Boston.

Five.

Once when my mother left my father for a few weeks, she called
to talk to my sister and me because, according to her, we were
both entitled to an explanation. "Your father," she said from a
motel in Nevada with a TV blaring in the background," is fucking
his secretary."

I was on the phone in the den, my sister was on one of the
upstairs extensions and my father was in the swimming pool with
a thin blond woman named Jill who was wearing one of my mother's bathing suits. Soon after the call, they got out of the pool,
dried off, and then the woman made us all tostadas in the kitchen.
I felt my sister's discomfort like a fifth presence at the table. I
watched her as she shredded her paper napkin into little pieces,
rolling those pieces into tiny balls, which then collected around
her chair.

The woman and my father talked about real-estate values in
West Los Angeles. She said she preferred living down on the
beach because she didn't have to keep her dog on a leash or
clean up after him when he pooped in the water. Pooped was
her word.

Later, my sister threw up her tostada in the shallow end of the pool and my father, who was always ineffectual when one of us was feeling sick, sent her upstairs to lie down.

Six.

Their dissolution had been just that, a slow dissolving; a couple dropping hands and moving in opposite directions. Part of it was the money. My father's promotion had been unexpected and premature, and their sudden affluence caught them by surprise. It made whatever plans they'd had from the beginning seem small and overly practical.

The marriage was a holdover from those early times they now regarded with embarrassment, much like the sofa bed that should not have made the trip to California with us. The day we moved in, it sat on the front lawn like a hick relative in ugly plaid, unwelcome.

Eventually, the money lubricated feelings; gifts were apologies, intended to divert attention elsewhere. I got my own phone when I picked up on a conversation I wasn't supposed to hear; the year my father got a new secretary, my mother got a sports car.

There were memories I held onto for a long time, until hindsight informed them and changed their meanings.

One afternoon from an upstairs window, I saw my parents out by the pool, lying side by side on chaises. I found their physical proximity comforting, a sign that everything was okay. My mother, still wet from a swim, was readjusting the straps of her suit and my father was bent over her, stretching to reach the radio, which sat on her other side, trying to fine tune the reception of the Rams game without getting up. Their faces almost touched. This casualness I read as a happy familiarity, a knowledge of each other that made conversation extraneous and excessive. Only years later did I realize it was a picture of indifference, not love.

Ultimately, cross purposes grew out of their having no purpose at all. The infidelity and malice had been afterthoughts, ways of making that drifting apart seem somehow intentional, charted.

Seven.

It is late August. We are taking the van to the beach because my father does not want us to get sand in the bottom of his Mercedes. Between my sister and me is a big Styrofoam ice chest that rubs against the vinyl seat and screeches. My mother tells us to put a towel between the chest and the seat, the noise drives her crazy.

Everything drives you crazy, my father says, and she laughs and kisses the back of his neck and says, You drive me crazy.

Meanwhile my sister and I are stealing grapes from the ice chest and spitting the seeds out the window, trying to hit street signs. To no one in particular I am listing the friends I want at my ninth-birthday party, which is several months away.

It's six o'clock, and we are driving along Sunset Boulevard, taking our dinner to the beach. This is always a last-minute idea on warm evenings, a postscript to days that have no direction: days spent waiting for someone to come fix the pool filter, spent playing balance beam on the brick retaining wall, spent making a layer cake from a Betty Crocker mix and putting blue food coloring in the icing.

My father asks if anyone's remembered to bring the blanket, and my sister giggles, Whoops, she left it on the hood of the other car in the garage. We're too close to the beach now to go back for it; it's about seven miles, and we all agree it's much nicer to sit directly on the sand anyway, especially when it's still keeping the day's heat. I say that if sand gets in the food it just tastes like a little bit of salt anyway, only crunchier, and everyone says, Yes, that's absolutely true.

We turn onto the Pacific Coast Highway, which runs as smooth and straight as a hemline between the beach and cliffs. It's a wide, fast highway, and my sister and I know it well enough to close our eyes and count the seconds between the lifeguard towers: one, two... tower sixteen... one, two, three... tower fifteen. And on and on.

The sun's almost gone by the time we swing left and into the empty parking lot behind tower eight—it's just a thumb of color above the horizon. The towers look strange and prehistoric in this light: small wooden platforms resting on long, storky metal legs.

We walk carefully across the parking lot because none of us is wearing shoes, and pick our way around pebbles and soda-can tabs and globs of tar. I run ahead with my sister and grab a good spot in between the stone breakers, a clean, flat area free of those small piles of cigarette butts and mounds of sand patted into headrests that make the beach look as if it has some kind of rash. We settle in: My mother unpacks the ice chest, laying food out on its cover, and my father points out places to my sister. That string of color is the Santa Monica Pier, and way off in the distance, see that pale gray line, that's Catalina Island. I'm sitting with my legs straight out in front of me, watching the sun set.

There are chicken sandwiches for dinner and plastic containers filled with potato salad and carrot salad. I don't eat the carrot salad because it's the kind with raisins and I hate raisins. We eat what's left of the grapes for dessert, and my mother says I'm silly because raisins are just dried grapes and I like grapes fine. I tell her taste isn't a logical thing, and knowing raisins are grapes doesn't make me like them any better. My parents laugh at that, and my father says I'm getting older, like he just this second realizes it, even though I've known it for a long time. By now, the sky is just long ribbons of color and the sun's gone.

My sister and I don't wait to digest dinner before going in the water because you can't really swim at night anyway—it's too cold and, besides, the way the dark waves open and snap like some wild animal frightens us. We dance in the water as it rushes up to our ankles. We pick shells and polished stones from the foam, dig for sand crabs after the water pulls back and leaves the sand glass-smooth, except for the dots of tiny air holes. My sister tells me that sand crabs are the only animals in the world that never sleep, and ones you see washed up on the beach are ones that fell asleep and drowned.

Then we're on a mission to climb the breakers. I'm ahead by a couple of feet, but my sister says there are huge sea snakes that hide in the rocks and that I'd better let her go first, just in case.

When we get to the top, we see a man and a woman on the stretch of beach before us. They're moving together, first back and forth, then up and down, the man doing push-ups with the woman underneath. My sister says that's making love, but I tell her it's not like that, it's more like dancing.

My father calls to us and we climb back down the large rocks, carefully, because it's easier to slip going down than coming up. Halfway to the ground my sister says, Look, and she pulls off her sweatshirt, lifting her elbow up to her head. Look, she says, pointing to a few hairs under her arm, as thin and light as cobwebs. I reach out to touch them, but she laughs and says it tickles, and then she's off, running, back through the water, kicking up foam.

I walk back slowly, and not through the water, but on the sand that's been hardened by the tide. Then I skip and gallop and hop, turning back to see which tracks are the strangest. It's the gallop, so I do that back to our spot.

They are packing up to leave. My mother is scraping the leftovers into a paper bag, which she hands to me with an empty wine bottle and points in the direction of a garbage can a few hundred feet down the beach. The sand has cooled now, is cold in fact, and I race to the can, which is buzzing with flies, and race back. My sister has already started to the van, lugging the large ice chest, her pant legs wet and frosted with sand.

My parents haven't moved. They're facing the other way, facing toward the water, which looks like a huge, dark mattress with a thin dust-ruffle of foam. They stand there saying nothing, my father's arm around my mother's shoulders and hers around his waist. My sister is at the van now and calling that the doors are locked and she has to go to the bathroom bad and that everyone had better hurry up. Her voice carries only as far as me, and I yell back to just shut up and pee behind the van, because I don't want my parents to be disturbed for a few more seconds. Another time I might run to be a part of this scene, cartwheeling into them so that they catch my legs, and hold me, splayed against them like a starfish. Or I might charge them like a bull, butting my head into the space between their two bodies, grinning crazily for added effect. Now, however, seems different; the picture of them alone together seems quite whole with me at a distance, just watching.

As I am walking back to the parking lot, I look up and see the houses on the cliffs high above the beach. They're huge white houses, and they're all lighted up and glowing, looking flat against the sky. The rains that have kept people sandbagging their property every winter have tugged at these houses, trying to drag them down to the water. Whole rooms hang out in the air, kitchens and living rooms, dangling hundreds of feet above the highway. Chunks of driveway pavement dribble down the cliffs. I've seen this sight before, many times, but every year the houses look closer to the edge, ready to tear apart and drop away with every rainstorm that takes a few more inches of the embankment.

I close my eyes and imagine sitting in some family room, watching TV and then, loud as thunder, there's a crack and a rumble and I'm slipping and trying to grab onto things that keep falling away: lamps, a coatrack, draperies.

My parents are at the car now. I point up to the cliffs and ask my father why people stay in these houses when, in a couple of years, there'll be nothing left but their front lawns.

My father says they stay because these are their *homes,* and then he climbs in behind the wheel and my mother slides over next to him. My sister and I fight about who gets to sit next to the good window, and that's the way we drive away, like any other family.

The rains cut deep, even gullies in the earth. From a distance, those white homes sat as proud and doomed as ancient capitals on fluted cliffs, and took longer than my first fifteen years to tumble in pieces into the sea.

Notes

The story behind the publication of "Private Lies" is a study in how a writer and an editor work together. Amy Lippman, who wrote the story as an undergraduate at Harvard, and Eileen Schnurr, fiction editor at *Mademoiselle,* shared a common vision of what the story was trying to achieve. They respected each other and had a good working relationship. But they also disagreed about a few things.

On the whole, Lippman says she's glad she got the chance to work with Schnurr. "I'm grateful that my first experience with an editor was with her. She understood what the story was about, what effect I was trying to achieve. . . . Eileen made the story better."

But while Lippman liked most of Schnurr's suggestions, there were two changes she didn't like. They involved only a few words near the end of the story, but Lippman felt they were important— important enough that she asked the original ending be used in this collection.

Lippman and Schnurr discussed the changes, but neither could change the other's mind. In the end, Schnurr prevailed.

Lippman says she was frustrated by the disagreements, but never seriously considered withdrawing the story. "I felt too young and inexperienced to pull it from *Mademoiselle.* It didn't seem productive to dwell on a sentence here or a sentence there.

"It just didn't feel like the right thing to do."

She doesn't regret her decision. "Essentially it *is* my story," she says.

Schnurr says the editing and rewriting that went into the publication of "Private Lies" is common. "Practically all the stories that get published in the magazine go through revisions. . . . This is a very important thing for writers to know. Writers see it as a sign of failure, whereas actually it's only the final step in the process."

The goal of that final step is not to change a story to meet an editor's wishes, she says. "I have no vested interest whatsoever in taking a story that has one point of view and turning it around. There is this feeling that editors want to commercialize stories and give them happy endings and that kind of thing—which absolutely is untrue."

Rather, the goal is to help authors realize their potential. "I spend a lot of time with writers going back and forth over all these things," Schnurr says. "Our aim is to develop the story to its absolute fullest and most satisfying."

The difficulties in the writing and editing of "Private Lies" arose in part from the effect Lippman was trying to produce. "The idea for the story began with its final image: Those houses that hang off the cliffs along the Southern California coast," Lippman says. "It was a powerful, frightening image from my childhood. . . . I saw those houses as a metaphor for what was happening to families around me. My story is about the different ways houses and homes fall apart."

The story also has another theme, though. "In another sense, it's about having to revise memories: a young woman looks back on her parents' divorce and, from the vantage of adulthood, begins to understand what happened," she says.

The format of the story—short segments that jump around in time—came about by accident. Lippman, who had been studying and writing poetry, first tried to work some of the story's images into a poem. "The result was more like indented prose than poetry, so I decided to try my hand at fiction," she says. "This is probably why the story was written in sections; the idea of writing a long story which could veer off in any direction was intimidating to me. I felt I could better control short, fragmented sections."

But the format serves the story well, she says. "It turned out this style was well suited to the subject since we remember experience in chunks, not in one long narrative."

She wrote the story in about two weeks. Several months later, she learned of *Mademoiselle's* Fiction Writers Contest, which is open to any writer eighteen to thirty years old whose fiction has never been published in a magazine with circulation of more than 25,000. She had a copy of "Private Lies" handy, so she sent it off.

She missed the contest's deadline, but the story caught Schnurr's eye. "It was very strong, spare, rich, sharp, beautifully controlled writing," Schnurr says. "It had a clearly distinctive voice behind it. Her voice in that story is her own. It doesn't sound like a million other stories."

So Schnurr wrote Lippman, telling her she could submit it for regular publication or save it for the next year's contest. Lippman waited, and won the contest the following year.

After she won, Lippman and Schnurr began preparing the story for publication.

Schnurr very much liked the story as originally written. "It evoked that disintegrating family in a beautiful way, so that she never told you anything absolutely directly. You lived in that story, you really felt everything that was happening."

But a few changes were needed, she says. "It was a tricky story in that it went back and forth in time. . . . At first it was more a series of scenes. It didn't have a real narrative idea connecting all the parts."

So she began working with Lippman. "She asked questions about the characters and their histories that made me rethink and rewrite several passages," Lippman says.

"For example, the first part of section two was written in response to Eileen's suggestion that I establish the narrator in the present day, looking back on her past." In that section, the narrator talks about the boxes of lamps and rugs her mother sends, about trying to find a place in her present life for all those pieces of her past.

Another suggestion from Schnurr sparked section six, where the narrator describes her parents' divorce as "a couple dropping hands and moving in opposite directions." Part of the problem, the narrator realizes now, was their sudden affluence. "It made whatever plans they'd had from the beginning seem small and overly practical," she says.

Schnurr "felt that the narrator had sufficient distance from her parents' break-up to offer some kind of explanation," Lippman says. That passage helps establish the narrative that was missing.

Lippman and Schnurr agreed on those changes, but disagreed on several others. Schnurr thought it was important that the reader know whose infidelity came first, the mother's or the father's. Lippman didn't. "It was a question I didn't want answered in the story. I thought that was something the narrator wouldn't want to address." Lippman won that one.

But Schnurr insisted on two other changes that Lippman didn't feel comfortable with. As originally published, the last section was introduced with these two sentences: "Some memories I haven't allowed myself to revise. I still believe in their accuracy."

"Eileen felt that this was a necessary preamble to the story's final section, the happy memory," Lippman says. "I disagreed. I wanted the reader to be jarred by the shift in tone and time and fought to do away with those two sentences."

The most significant change, though, was the ending. The final paragraph was cut before publication in *Mademoiselle*, so that the story ended like this: "My father says they stay because these are their *homes*, and then he climbs in behind the wheel and my mother slides over next to him. My sister and I fight about who gets to sit next to the good window, and that's the way we drive away, like any other family."

Lippman says, "Perhaps because that last image was where the whole story began for me, I felt its inclusion was critical. Without it, the story seemed to trail off. I didn't like the ironic tone of 'we drive away, like any other family'—in part because the other passages seem to end on a similar note. I wanted the story to really *end.*"

Schnurr says she and the other editors at *Mademoiselle* were unanimous in wanting what she describes as "a kind of poetic evocation" at the end cut. "It was extraneous. The story really properly ended at the point where we ended it. It's just an editorial instinct, but we saw that these lines diminished the dramatic effect."

Despite their disagreement, Schnurr and Lippman maintained a good working relationship. Lippman says having an honest difference of opinion with her editor didn't spoil her first publication experience. "I was thrilled to have won the contest, and very happy to be published in *Mademoiselle*. Overall, it was a very positive experience."

Sunday

Someone knocked at the door. This was no very strange event. There were always salesmen or children knocking on the door. Sometimes when the door was opened, no one was there. Sometimes the door opened for no reason and stood ajar until someone from inside noticed and closed it.

Someone knocked at the window. Myra lifted her eyebrows at Joe. But her coffee was so delicious, so strong and fresh, that she didn't move.

Breakfast was for them a precious and prolonged luxury. Myra made the best banana bread, heavy and sweet, in the Four Corners region. They both knew this. This and the coffee, this and the cream cheese, this and the very joy of being together and alone, was too much to abandon to a knock at the door or window.

And this was Sunday. Joe knew that Sunday there is no mail, no work, no stock exchange. Sunday is nothing but empty air. Maybe they'd hear from Joe Junior. He was in the Navy and liked to call every Sunday at 1100 hours. Their younger boy Henry was a Pentecostal minister. He never called. Sometimes Myra had nightmares about Henry. He appeared in a highbacked chair with a sword in his lap, his hair blown back by a wind of unknown source. He smiled. Over and over he said, "Bya ya ya." Myra shook her head and held her hands out for him. But he vanished, or became a turtle, and she realized she was at the bottom of a lake. A cow carcass hovered a few feet above her, tangled in fishing line.

Her dreams were flimsy like memories, though not as familiar. She remembered calling the boys in for dinner one night. Joe Junior, nearly identical to Joe Senior, rushed to the table and held the mashed potato bowl in his hands, suspending his face over its steam. Myra called louder for Henry. Nothing. She checked his bedroom. The boys' bathroom. The front yard. The back. She found him lying on his stomach behind the dwarf oleanders. He wore a sheet folded into a lumpy loincloth.

"What's this all about, Henry?" She nudged him with her toe.

"I want to be like Christ." He held himself rigid while she struggled to pick him up.

"Henry, stop it. What would Miss Hickman say if she saw this?" He adored Miss Hickman, who by a twist of fate and a teacher shortage had been his second, third, and fourth grade teacher. This was the best tactic Myra could muster, and it never failed.

"She would marry me and help me do the work of the Lord." Myra pulled him up and dusted him off. She refused to let him eat dinner dressed as the crucified Christ.

Joe tapped the table with his knife. She was out of cream cheese, so she opened a jar of marmalade and dropped a few spoonfuls on his bread. He read aloud the possibilities offered by the television schedule. Myra enjoyed the last cup of coffee. She noticed that she'd chipped the nail of her right ring finger.

Joe liked a good game of golf. So his day was decided. A scotch and water, two of them perhaps, the old armchair soft with the imprint of his body, and golf. And Myra should sit beside him.

As for Myra, she knew that her sister Louise's apricots would go to waste if they were not immediately folded into a cobbler. She gave Joe a quick kiss. The back doorknob rattled. She ignored it.

So Myra baked a cobbler. Joe breathed the apricot air and sipped his second scotch. The telephone rang and Joe almost rose to answer it, but he felt that little twinge in his back. He waited to see if Myra would pick it up, though he knew she wouldn't. After a few rings the answering machine took the call. It was Joe Junior. He'd phone again next week.

Myra loaded the dishwasher and made a second pot of coffee. The old percolator seemed almost too heavy to hold when it was as full as she liked it.

She sat alone in the kitchen and lifted the cup of black coffee to her face. She flipped through her recipe file. It was like a diary. Here was that horrible marshmallow cake. And the rum punch she'd made for their tenth anniversary. And here was Henry's favorite, chicken spinach roll. She hadn't cooked it for years, not since his last dinner at home. She had made all his favorites, and tried not to say anything unpleasant. But when he held his hands over his milk and looked heavenward, Myra leaned toward him and asked, "Who told you these things? How did you get these ideas?"

Henry answered that without the grace of God he would have known nothing of his spirit. He was perfectly composed, and punctuated his sentences with his right hand, waving it evenly like a baton. She could not disengage her eyes from that baton. Soon she heard only a garbled and unlikely combination of sounds. She watched his hand, up and down. Beside her Joe was buttering his hard roll, and would in a moment hurl it at his son.

They understood each other, she and Joe. They shared much of everything pleasant. Now Myra was mixing tuna salad. Joe was watching Sunday golf. He toyed with a small malachite pig from Myra's pig collection. Myra heard the regular squeaks of his armchair as he rocked from side to side.

It did, of course, occur to her sometimes that she knew nothing of Henry's condition or whereabouts. There had been a show on television, a documentary. Joe held her hand while they watched a preacher rest his plump and placid fingers on an old woman's head. Behind him a row of girls shifted their eyes between the healing and the television camera. They wore identical braids and various sizes of identical brown dresses. There was some shouting. The woman's eyes grew into large and empty opals. Joe pulled his hand from Myra's and waved the remote control toward the screen. They were able to catch the end of a trout-fishing competition.

After lunch Myra joined Joe by the television. She intended to write some letters.

There was a rap on the door. Myra squinted at the golf. Another knock followed. She waved her hand in irritation toward it.

She wrote to Louise to thank her for the fruit. She tried to write a cheery letter, with a special adjective for the apricots. She tried "tangy" and "tempting," but crossed them out. Then she filed down her chipped nail, but this made her other nails seem too long. She filed them all.

For dinner Myra made a simple casserole of vegetables and beef, a hint of garlic, a sprinkle of parsley. She burned her arm on the oven door and made a strange sound, not a scream, more like a groan, which embarrassed her. But the casserole went over well. Joe nudged her feet under the table. His eyeglasses were white with steam.

As Myra cleared the table she noticed a barely audible, rhythmic thumping coming from one of the walls. It was soft and almost comforting. She listened for a moment, then placed her palm flat against the wall. There it was. Dull, but distinct.

It was a little like the mumbling. When Henry was a teenager, Myra used to press her ear against his door. She never caught a word clearly, but she knew the tone of voice of prayer. One night she opened the door. He was in bed. His desk lamp was on above an elementary algebra text. His mouth was open and his tongue moved slightly when he inhaled. She straightened his sheet and smoothed a place to sit beside him. She felt his forehead. She wanted to speak through his sleep, to say, "Henry, I'm your mother, don't you know? I made you."

But where was she? It was Sunday night. The pleasant day was closing every moment. It was time for the TV movie. Joe brought her a sherry. Myra took little sips and held them in her mouth until they were smooth enough to swallow. She tried to remember a recipe she'd known many years before, a sherry sauce for pork. On the screen a happy Texas family was wrenched from its moorings by a drop in beef prices. Myra wondered why she'd cut down their meat consumption. Joe was thin. They were perfectly healthy.

A while later someone knocked on the door. She stopped to look at it. But Joe was already mounting the stairs. He turned back to her with eyes that said "It's time." She waited a minute, but followed him. She let the faded, familiar sheets close around her. They felt like her pastry apron, and she fed her boys from its pocket.

Notes

"Sunday" is the exception that proves the rule. It has no dialogue and no real plot. The characters are somewhat flat and undeveloped. The setting and time are very vague.

And yet it works.

"You're taught there has to be dialogue and action, and this story has very little of those things," says Cecelia Hagen of the *Northwest Review*. "Not much happens. But the way it *doesn't* happen is what's interesting."

By using what doesn't happen, Regina Marler reveals the underlying pain that motivates her characters, Hagen says. "She shows the pressure they never address with the dream the mother has and the knocking and the telephone ringing. They have this kind of willed complacency about their lives. . . . The pain they don't allow themselves to feel propels all this domesticity."

Regina Marler did not start out to write "Sunday." "My intention was to write a story called 'Doors, Windows, and Coffee,' in which these items represent three stages of domestic dissatisfaction in the lives of Joe and Myra," she recalls. But when she began the story, she found she had written "an unexpectedly odd first paragraph." Within a few lines the story became something entirely different from what she had begun.

"I think it was the unplanned appearance of Henry, who immediately took control and became a tool for exposing Myra, that changed the story into 'Sunday.' "

Once she discovered what she wanted to write, Marler says, she was very careful not to spell everything out for the reader. "People's varying interpretations of the story are always interesting to hear, and convince me of the richness and independence of the written word . . . ," she says. "Most people ask me what 'the knocking' is (some demand to know), and are frustrated to hear that I have no more to say about the story than what is written on the page. Plurality of interpretations pleases me—if people invent or perceive a meaning separate from mine, then the story is effective."

One way she did that was by keeping her characters undeveloped. "My characters are intentionally two-dimensional and inhabit not 'the' world, but simply 'a' world, and I hesitate to flesh them out realistically with background details, to give them lives other than the narrow life of this story," she says.

Hagen points out that the characters aren't completely flat, though. She says Myra's dream in the fourth paragraph, where she sees Henry in a high-backed chair and then finds herself at the bottom of a lake with a cow carcass tangled in fishing line overhead, is crucial to the story.

"Maybe if the mother didn't have that dream you'd see their complacency, but would there be enough of a hint of what's underneath that complacency and what that complacency is denying for us to sense it? You can't just write about boring people—that's boring. If she didn't have the dream, I don't think the story would have worked. Myra *is* a two-dimensional character but you see that there's this side to her life, this subconscious that's nothing like TV golf and trout-fishing competition."

Hagen says Marler tackled a difficult job when she chose to write about characters who repress their feelings because she had to show many things the characters themselves weren't conscious of. "It's similar to the problems where the main character is a child. You don't want the story to be strictly limited to an eight-year-old's view, and yet you don't want this eight-year-old thinking adult thoughts because then you'll lose credibility."

Hagen also likes the way Marler treated Joe and Myra. "She was not ridiculing or sanctimonious towards her characters, even though she was distant from them. Often writers will belittle their characters, or write a story and there's no one in it that's likeable. That's a very hard thing to pull off. But here you feel sorry for these people, and it's because the writer treats them so gently."

The story's simplicity works in its favor, Hagen says. "It doesn't have a huge grasp and it doesn't cover centuries. It is very small," she admits. "But we liked the unpretentiousness of it. As one editor said, 'A simple thing done well is much better than a complex thing done poorly.'"

Even though the editors at *Northwest Review* liked the story right away, they asked Marler for some revisions before they accepted it. Hagen suggested that she smooth some transitions, make the dream scene more vivid, and change one sentence where the point of view changed to Joe's.

"Although I was eager to publish, if I had disagreed with her comments, I would not have altered the story," Marler says. "As it was, I trusted her vision of the story, which, while it differed from mine, seemed to complement what I was working toward. The story was definitely better after revision."

Marler did reject one suggestion. Hagen recommended that she expand the scene where Myra tries to get Henry to behave by mentioning his teacher, Miss Hickman, to show other instances where that tactic had worked. Marler didn't agree, saying she didn't want to expand those characters' lives beyond the limited scope of the story. Hagen says her reasoning made sense, and showed that Marler had really thought through her story, so she accepted her decision.

"Her work impressed us because she had taken our considerations and suggestions and really done a good job with them," Hagen says. "And because she didn't just do everything we said."

The editors at *Northwest Review* suggested one final change after the revised draft was submitted—that the original title of "Sunday is Nothing But Empty Air" be shortened to "Sunday."

Appropriate. A simple title for a simple story.

Or is it a simple story, after all?

Among the Righteous

A D.C. woman can be a hard-headed woman, and so Odis Renfro, newly released from his job as janitor, stock clerk, and general handyman at Speidell's Auto Parts Warehouse, pauses on the Avenue, two blocks from home, thinking of how best to tell his wife. Like Odis himself, the Avenue has seen better days. The fronts of the stores are faded, and the window of the laundromat on the corner is held together by a bolted square of plywood. Across the street, the barber Lamar Jenkins stands in the window of his shop, one eye on the Avenue, the other on the head of the customer in his chair. He waves, but Odis does not see him.

Nearby, several men stand in the shade of Cohen's Liquor Store, sharing a sullen useless fierceness. One, different from the others—he has only one good eye and, better-dressed, sports yellow, round-toed shoes with high heels—says, "I'ma tell y'all the truth." His other eye is milky-white, a dead pearl; he cocks his head, favoring his good eye, and for a moment Renfro thinks the one-eyed man is looking at him.

The one-eyed man says, "Ain't nothin' mess over a man worse than to let a bitch get hol' of his min'." The men's laughter comes, profane and emptily profound. Another, standing near the gutter, elbows on the square blue trash receptacle, says, "Preach it Night Train. A bitch mess up yo' min' in a minit!"

And Renfro goes on, a tall, stoop-shouldered man in green khaki pants and a matching jacket with his first name, Odis, embroidered in red letters over the left pocket, still thinking of what Daisy will say.

At supper, Renfro finds his wife demanding he do something about the shoes their oldest son, Wallace, is wearing. The boy, almost thirteen, had bought them that same day with money earned from his paper route. The shoes have round toes and chunky high heels and are in fashion that spring among the jobless young and not-so-young men who line the Avenue from late morning until long after midnight. For that reason, Daisy Renfro thinks them unseemly for the son of a deacon at the One Faith United Baptist Church.

After seeing the shoes, Odis agrees, although they remind him—in spirit, if not shape—of a knob-toed, patent leather pair with thin soles he himself had bought when it was still important no one know how recently he had come from the South.

"Well," he says slowly to the boy. "You got the receipt?"

Wallace nods sullenly, looking down at his plate and his half-eaten dinner. His brother, Wilson, five years younger, pushes his glasses up on his nose as he looks from his father to Wallace and back to his father again. The glasses, round and wire-rimmed, came from the clinic. They are always falling down. Both boys are cocoa brown, but Wallace is sharp-featured with darting eyes that size up and appraise, while Wilson, his face still pudgy with baby fat, gazes about him serenely but intently, as if looking past the surface of things to some deeper meaning.

"Good," Odis says. "You ain't wore 'em that long. I guess you can take 'em back and get your money."

"Why?" Wallace says.

"Because," Odis replies, "I said so."

When Wallace says nothing, Odis motions for Daisy to pass him the bowl of greens. He dumps a spoonful on his plate, sets the bowl pointedly in front of Wallace—who has managed to get through the meal without taking any—and begins to eat again, nodding at Daisy as if the matter has been settled. Daisy purses her lips and looks doubtful.

"Why I gotta take 'em back?" Wallace says. He starts in a deep bass and ends in a high squeak; his voice is changing. He frowns, sticking out his lower lip as he looks defiantly at Odis. "I paid for 'em with my own money."

Odis chews without haste and swallows. He sets his fork down and rests his elbows on the table, looking over his folded hands at the boy. Daisy sighs from the other end of the table.

"Wallace, have some greens," she says. "And Wilson, eat your dinner. Times hard enough without you wastin' food in this house. Plenty of people be glad to have what you left lyin' there." The spoon clinks against the china as Wallace takes a small helping of greens and Daisy looks half warningly, half imploringly at Odis. "Odis. . . ."

"Because they ain't no kinda shoes for a boy like you to be wearin'," Odis says with an exaggerated, fraudulent patience that means he has heard enough. "You'da wanted to buy you some shoes, you shoulda bought some like them school shoes your momma bought you in September."

Wallace sweeps his arm over the table in a gesture that dismisses sturdy oxfords and all sensible things. "Them ain't no kinda shoes," he says disdainfully, and Wilson giggles. "Them baby shoes. I want me some shoes like a man wear, not no shoes for a schoolboy."

"Well, what you think you is?" Odis levels his forefinger at the boy. "You gon' take back them shoes. First thing after school tomorrow. You gon' take back them shoes . . . or my name ain't Odis Renfro."

"Uh uh," Wallace says under his breath.

"Whatchu say?" Odis thunders.

"Uh uh," the boy says. "I ain't gon' do it."

Odis stands, tearing the napkin from his neck in one swift motion. The boy starts, pushing back his chair so that it clatters to the floor. After a moment, he bends to pick it up. His eyes never leave his father's stony face. "Odis," Daisy pleads, but the two of them glare at each other—one defiant, the other overcome with anger at that defiance—each with the same high forehead and jutting, determined jaw. Wallace shakes his head once.

"Uh uh," he says again.

"Awright," Odis says. "We gon' see about that," and he yanks the boy upstairs, straps him several times with his own belt, and watches as he gets into bed.

Odis comes downstairs muttering that he is still the man in the house, he puts the meat on the table and the clothes on their backs and, by God, he is going to be respected. Daisy and Wilson finish the meal looking at their plates. It is the first time Odis has struck either of the boys.

Shortly before five o'clock that Tuesday, Speidell, a bull-necked white man with a mush-mouth Tidewater Virginia accent, had asked Odis to put the CLOSED sign in the window of the Grand Prix Auto Parts Warehouse and step back into the office. There, amid cartons stacked waist-high on the floor and belts of various sizes hanging from nails in the walls, Speidell removed a box of sparkplugs from his chair and sat down behind the desk.

Odis remained standing.

Speidell said that after almost seventeen years he knew Odis would understand. It wasn't that he didn't need him, and it wasn't that Odis wasn't a good worker. It was just that times, as Odis surely knew, were hard and, until they got better, he was just going to have to try to keep the store going by himself.

Odis almost dropped the cap he had been turning in his hands. All he could think to do was say he understood. Speidell, obviously relieved, took a folded-over check from his shirt pocket, gave it to Odis, and shook his hand.

When Odis looked while waiting for the bus, he noted that the check was for two weeks, three days more than he had worked. He buttoned it away in his shirt pocket, grudgingly grateful, but he knew that once the money was gone he would be unable to do the one thing a man should be able to do—support his family.

By the time he tells Daisy about it after they have gone upstairs to bed, Odis is mad. He is mad at Speidell for letting him go after seventeen years where he has hardly missed a day, mad at the conditions he does not fully understand that have made it necessary, and he is mad at himself because he knows he lost his temper with Wallace only because he had been laid off.

"Of course I *know* times is hard" Odis says fiercely, keeping his voice low so as not to wake the two boys asleep in the room across the hall. "That Speidell don't know nothin' 'bout hard. Let him come live this side of town like we do, he wanna learn somethin' 'bout it."

"Uh huh," Daisy says in vague assent, and turns to the window. The light from the street shines through a place where the curtains do not quite meet, showing the paper curlers twisted throughout her greying hair. A man and a woman pass underneath the open window, their footsteps and laughter echoing after they have gone. Two blocks away, on the Avenue, an ambulance siren slashes the air.

Odis stands and closes the window. He has light brown skin and hair that is cut close on the sides and thinning on top. Silhouetted against the window, he is as thin as he was in the gold-framed wedding picture on the dresser. People who do not know them well think he is younger than Daisy.

"That all he said?" she asks, patting the top of the bedside table, searching for her glasses. "He didn't say nothin' 'bout how long?"

"Naw." Odis sits heavily on the bed. "You know how he is. If I ast him, he say—"

The floor in the hall outside their bedroom creaks and Daisy raises herself from where the mattress sags towards the center and turns on the light. She has wide shoulders and heavy arms under her nightgown. "Wilson?" she calls. "Which onea you boys is that?"

"Wallace, ma'am," he squeaks.

"What you doin' up? Tomorrow's a school day."

"I ain't *up*," Wallace says gruffly. "I just had to get me a drink of water."

"Boy," Odis says, starting to rise, "don't you sass your—" but Daisy has her hand on his shoulder.

"Well, get it then," she says. "And get right to bed. You hear?" She turns to plump her pillow and then settles back against it, not waiting for the boy's response.

Odis says, "You know if I was to ast him, all Speidell say is he can't say."

Daisy sighs. "I worry about that boy," she says. "You was too rough on him tonight."

"Ain't nothin' wrong with him, 'cept his head still hard. But I guess you right—I ain't had to do all that to let him know just 'cause he wear long pants and can buy his own shoes don't make him a man."

"You know I'm right." Daisy looks at him over her glasses and Odis looks away. He shifts, starts to get up, and then lies down again. It is on her face that they have been putting it off and can afford to do so no longer.

"You know we can't make it on what we got saved," Daisy says. "Not for long."

Odis passes his hand over his jaw, making a small scratching sound on the stubble. He shifts uneasily on the bed so that he and Daisy slide closer to each other.

"I know it," he says softly. "I didn't figure it exactly, but I knew it. But what else am I gon' do, 'cept go out and look for another job? Times is hard, just like the man said."

"You could go back and tell the man he cain't fire you," Daisy says.

Odis swings his head to look at her. Her tone was so deliberate and the answer so quick that he knows she must have come on it while listening when he told her what Speidell had said before giving him the check. Daisy looks back at him, brown eyes calm and unwavering, and Odis turns away, asking himself what in the world he has done to deserve such a hard-headed woman.

"Speidell just did what he had to do," he says mildly, hoping to persuade her before she latches too firmly onto the idea. "I know he'll give me a good reference. Business been bad all last year. Unemployment is high. It ain't all his fault."

"Didn't say it was," Daisy says. "But as long as you worked for that man, he owe you more than, 'Sorry Odis, but I got to let you go.' You got a wife and two children to feed. You got house payments to make and bills to pay. Just like he do. Go tell him that."

While he thinks of what to say to her, Odis thinks of the patent leather shoes he once owned. He was not yet married then, and he had been working for Speidell for about six months. He was never without money. There were mornings he came to work having slept only two or three hours, the taste of gin still in his mouth. He had worn the shoes to dancehall and poolroom until the leather veneer began to split, showing the cheap cardboard underneath. He had never bought another pair, because shortly afterwards he met Daisy and realized—it was one of her first questions—that he had not been to church since leaving home.

"I can't do that," Odis says. "Every day for the past seven*teen* years I gone in there and work' for that man. He can't treat me no better, I'll get me another job. Might even take my time, till I find what I want. I could use a few days rest."

He can feel her disbelief, as solid and as real as her body beside him. The truth is, Speidell *does* owe him more than a handshake and three days' extra pay. But he cannot do what she is saying. The galling humiliation of such an appeal is not all that prevents Renfro from denying it possibilities. More simply, he cannot imagine himself confronting Speidell with the proper impassive inevitability. This he does not tell Daisy.

"Awright." Daisy sets her glasses on the table and flicks off the light. "But bills not gon' stop comin' just 'cause you restin'," she says, turning and settling to give Odis the broad expanse of her back. "What you gon' do then?"

"I don't know, woman," Odis says. "But right now, I'm gon' try and get me some sleep."

There are, besides those who must eat in the Renfro household, payments on the house itself and other bills that arrive with the impersonal regularity of first and fifteenth. These are the things a man must see to. For the next several mornings, Renfro rises early to ride the bus, clutching folded-over pages from the want ads with whole columns circled.

After watching him return mute in the afternoons with a pocketful of useless, hoarded transfers, Daisy can no longer refrain.

"You fin' anything?" she asks at dinner.

Odis shakes his head. "Not yet. But it's only a matter of time before I get lucky."

By now, of course, the boys know, and so Daisy determines to wait.

"You know," she says brightly, "I saw Mrs. Granger this afternoon. She stop' me on the street and tell me she hit the number. Just had to tell all she was gon' do with that money."

"That right," Odis says.

"She say she win three hundred dollars. Played seven-six-one."

Odis, looking at Wallace, says, "Boy, you take back them shoes?"

"Uh huh," Wallace says.

"Watchu mean 'uh-huh'? Yes or no?"

"Odis," Daisy says, and Wilson says, "He took 'em back, Poppa."

"Awright." Odis says, to Daisy, "Well, Miz Granger sure is lucky."

"That's right." Daisy stands to clear the table. "Luck will take care of you. But you can't count on it all the time."

They sit downstairs after the boys have gone to bed. Daisy sews a patch on a pair of Wilson's jeans. Odis looks at the newspaper, searching the empty narrow columns in the back of the sports pages.

Finally, Daisy turns the pants to the light and draws the needle through. "You go to Speidell?" she says.

"Naw." Odis raises the paper to hide his face even more. "What kind of man am I gon' look like, go beggin' Speidell for my job?"

Daisy knots the thread and raises it to her mouth so she can bite off the end. Sticking the needle into the pincushion on the table beside her, she turns the pants to the next hole and adjusts the patch. She fixes it with pins and takes up the needle again.

"'A haughty spirit go before a fall,'" she says at last. "Least, that's what the Book say. Or did you forget?"

When Odis makes no response, Daisy sets down her sewing.

"Why you have to be so stubborn, Odis? It ain't for me I want you to go back there. You see me runnin' around wearin' jewelery and fancy clothes, goin' to the beauty shop every weekend? We ain't even got a *car*. But I want us to own this house for the boys, and I want to put somethin' away for them, so they can go further in this life than we did. Go talk to the man, Odis."

"Lemme tell you somethin'," Odis says, putting down the paper. His voice is trembling. "My daddy thought you had to be that way. He'd step off a sidewalk and grin, 'cause that's what you had to *do* just to get by down there. Me, soon as I was old enough, I caught the first thing smokin' and come up here. Speidell don't want me, I'll go where somebody else do. I learned a long time ago you can't always win. But least you can go where you don't have to fight every day."

Daisy squints at her sewing and stabs the cloth with her needle. Odis turns the page, making the newspaper crackle.

"I wouldn't know anything about that," she says.

"You never *had* to, not livin' up here."

In a little while Daisy sets down the sewing and takes off her glasses.

"I'm goin' to bed," she says. And when Odis does not move, "You comin', Mr. Renfro?"

Odis folds the paper and sets it down.

"Yeah," he says wearily. "I'm comin'."

On the afternoon of another grey day of worry, Odis Renfro eats with a slow abstractedness that precludes enjoyment, pours himself a second cup of coffee, listening as he sips it to the vigorous thumps of Daisy upstairs.

These days he no longer goes out. They have become akin to Saturdays, but empty, without mornings for him to take hammer and saw and, with sure brown hands, set about the tasks she has saved for him. In the end, there would be the rich evidence of a thing set right and well-made. And afterwards, the slow walk to the church, floors to wax and polish, pews to dust in the still holiness of the sanctuary. And then the fine solace of the barber-shop and the balm of Lamar Jenkins' hands, laughter and cigar smoke and the nimble swapping of lies, small sips in the back room from a bottle covered by a brown paper bag. And finally, on Saturdays, home, dinner, and sometimes—more rarely now—the sweetness of coaxing Daisy's body from the cocoon of its stolidity, a mutual easing with shy wonder and circumspection; the boys sleep in the room next door.

Odis goes to the landing and calls: "C'mon down and have some coffee wid' me, sugar. Pot still warm."

Another thump and Daisy comes, balancing a wicker basket against one hip, says, passing without stopping so that he must yield the way: "Four people's dirty clothes and sheets to wash and iron and I'm late gittin' started. I ain't got time to siddown." She looks at him pointedly. " 'Less you gon' help with the laundry."

It is then that Odis Renfro decides to go to the barbershop.

Lamar Jenkins looks up from dusting rows of multi-colored lotions, oils, and ointments, trying to hide his surprise when Renfro walks in. Odis tosses his cap on the hatrack. He sits and says, with a heartiness he does not feel, "Afternoon, Mr. Jenkins. Guess I'll take my usual today." The two men are alone in the shop.

Jenkins gives the bottles one last flick before he sets down the duster and adjusts his green eyeshade. He lowers the chair, winds the tissue paper around Odis' neck, sweeps a clean striped cloth over his knees, draws it up under his chin. Pinning it, he pats him once on the shoulder and turns to select clippers. Odis, looking out the window, can see the men on the corner. And then Jenkins begins, and he closes his eyes under the soft, soothing hum.

"You in kinda early," Jenkins says "Take off from work?"

"More like it took off from me. Los' my job."

Jenkins stops, holding the clippers away from Odis' neck.

"You kiddin' me, man. Down at the auto parts store?"

"Thass right."

"Man." Jenkins shakes his head and lowers the clippers again. "After all them years, thass a hell of a note. What you gon' do now, Deacon?"

Odis thinks about the day Speidell called him into the back room.

He says, "Keep lookin'."

Jenkins considers this. Once, there were two other barbers, the three chairs filled and a long-headed boy or a woman with slick hair waiting, but now, with the passing of each first of the month, Jenkins, uncomplaining, has time to look out at the Avenue. He turns the chair for better perspective on the grey horseshoe of hair over which Odis has granted him custody. He says, "You fin' something, Deacon. Jus' a matter of time."

Odis says nothing. The barbershop smells of bay rum and powder, and the hum of the clippers is as comforting as rain on a tin roof. He could go to sleep in the peace of the enameled steel chair's cracked leather.

"Daisy awright?"

"Takin' it bad. I just wish somebody hadda tol' me when I come up here that a DeeCee woman is a *hard-headed* woman."

Jenkins chuckles, and Odis says, "Tell the truth, it's my boy I'm worried about. Wallace come home the other night with some shoes."

"Shoes? What kinda shoes?"

"I don't know whatchu call 'em. Got round toes and high heels. Bottoms look like they an inch thick. Say he don't want no schoolboy shoes. Then he sass me at the dinner table—his momma sittin' right there. I took him upstairs and showed him whose house he livin' in."

Jenkins laughs softly under his breath. Odis laughs too, and Jenkins says, without reproach, "You too hard on that boy, Odis. How old he now? Fifteen? Sixteen?"

"Shoot, he ain't but workin' on thirteen. But I guess you right—I ain't had to do all that to let him know just 'cause he wear long pants and think he got somethin' to put in 'em, that don't make him a man."

In the silence that follows, Odis thinks of the shoes he himself once owned. More than once, he had shambled to his rented room drunk in them. Until the veneer had split and the repairman to whom he took them pointed out the cardboard underneath, his tone making it clear Odis had been a fool. It was shortly after that he met Daisy and, without undue struggle, surrendered.

Jenkins finishes, shutting off the clippers for the last time, prepares the towel dusted with talcum powder, and Odis, reluctant to leave the security of the chair for the new-found hazards of home, asks for a shave. "Thass extra," Jenkins says automatically, and Odis nods; both men have known for a long time.

The barber is lathering his face, looking from time to time out the window, when he stops.

"Deacon," he says, and in his voice there is that he does not believe what he is seeing. "Look out the window. Ain't that your boy?"

When Odis sits up, he sees Wallace, wearing the new shoes he has been told to return, taking out cigarettes and handing them around to the men on the corner. Wilson stands nearby. Halfway to the door, Odis remembers the cloth around his neck. He tears it off, scattering the safety pin to the floor. Jenkins comes out after him, holding the shaving brush.

"Boy, whatchu doin' out here?" Odis growls, and Wallace puts the cigarettes behind his back. He looks at Odis defiantly, and from between sullen lips comes the word, "Nothin'."

The one-eyed man smiles, stroking his chin with a furtive slyness as he regards Odis' mad-dog face. His companions smile too, but Odis is looking at his boys. Wilson shifts from foot to foot, as if he has to go to the bathroom and is waiting for someone to notice.

"Poppa?" Wilson says, pulling at Odis' arm. Odis bends to listen. "Wallace jus' tryin' to git his money. He been givin' Night Train his lunch money to play the number for him."

Odis looks wonderingly at Jenkins over the boy's head. Jenkins looks as if he wants to laugh, and Odis stands.

"That right?" he says mildly.

Wallace nods. "Played seven-six-one," he says. "Jus' like Miz Granger. Won me almost a hundred dollars." And then, "Somebody got to be the man in the house and bring home some money."

Jenkins, still trying not to laugh, says, "You give your money to this man? This man here?"

Wallace says, "Night Train, that's his name."

And the laughter that has been bubbling inside Jenkins explodes, and the barber with the wet brush soaking the pocket of his smock throws back his head and laughs. Odis permits himself a thin smile.

"Night Train?" Jenkins chokes out. "He call hisself that now? When he first come up here from Arkansaw—an' had enough money to come in my shop—somebody give him that name. Say he look like he only got one headlight—"

"—An' he so clumsy you can hear him comin' in the dark," Odis finishes, and the two men laugh, deep, full, rich laughter, the laughter that still comes Saturday night in the barbershop, when they remember that once they were young and the nights endless, and it was nothing to wake up with the taste of gin in their mouths and go out again, because it was the thing to do, to earn their bread.

"Man . . . ," Night Train starts, reaching for his pocket, and Wallace looks down at his new shoes. Wilson looks once at Night Train, and then he nods to himself.

These, Odis thinks, are his boys, both his boys that are so different. All at once he knows that if God granted him one wish, it would not be for himself or Daisy, but that each of his sons could exchange what was lacking in him for what the other had in abundance, that Wallace's mindless enthusiasm might be tempered with Wilson's caution, that Wilson would become more bold. And because this cannot be so, he knows there is only a little while for his love to protect them.

He says, to Night Train, "When I was a young man, I took care of myself with my fists and my feet. But I'm too old to fight now, and too proud to run. So I carry a friend in my pocket, and what I keep says you gon' give my boy back his lunch money."

Now the other men drift away, as if heeding a call only they can hear. Night Train studies Odis' face. After a long moment, he says, "Cain't argue with that," and pulls out three crumpled dollar bills. He starts to hand them to Odis, but Odis says, "No," and Night Train gives them to Wallace.

The boys turn, ready to go, but Odis is not quite finished.

"Now," he says. "Numbers man, huh?" He looks at each of the boys. "Lemme tell you somethin'. You don't have to go lookin' for a numbers man, a *real* numbers man. A real numbers man come lookin' for *you*. 'Cause all he got is his word, and it's bad for business if people start sayin' you can't pay off."

Finished, he looks at Wallace. "Come here," he says gently.

And when the boy comes, he puts his arm around his shoulders, pointing at Night Train's retreating figure. He says, softly, so only Wallace can hear, "You think thass all there is to bein' a man?" and when the boy does not answer, swats him twice across the seat of the pants. The tears spring hotly to Wallace's eyes, but Odis ignores them.

"Go on," he says. "Tell yo momma I be home soon." And to Wilson, who stands looking up at his father, "You too. And don't let me catch y'all out here again."

Later, standing behind the chair, Jenkins says, with the deference due a man he has seen with a woman not his wife, "Deacon, I didn't know you carried a piece," and Odis reaches under the cloth to take out key ring and coins, and a penknife no bigger than his thumb.

"Huh," Jenkins says. And then, "He be awright. You got a good boy there. 'N' you raisin' him right. Gon' grow up to make you proud."

"Yeah," Odis says. "If I don't wear out his behind first."

That evening, lying on the couch reading the newspaper, Deacon Odis Renfro looks up often, chuckling softly to himself, once even raising his hand and wiping his eyes. Daisy turns her sewing and looks over at him with familiar suspicious tolerance. She frowns.

"Well," Odis says after a while. "Guess I get up early tomorrow and go talk to Speidell."

"Good." Daisy sticks the needle in the pincushion, searches in the pool of mending in her lap for some item small enough to complete before bedtime. "I knew you'd do right."

"How you know?" Odis says.

" 'Cause," Daisy says. "I wouldn't never of married you—let alone *stayed* for seventeen years—if I didn't know you could see it when you wrong."

D A V I D   N I C H O L S O N

· ·

103

Notes

When Odis Renfro, still thinking about the knob-toed patent leather shoes of his youth, took a belt to his son for the first time and returned to the dinner table muttering about being the man of the house, I knew what kind of man Odis was. He felt powerless after being fired and, much like his thirteen-year-old son, was struggling to be treated like a man. But he also remembered the days of patent leather and gin, and knew what it was like to be on the verge of manhood. And he remembered when he exchanged those days for life with a hard-headed D.C. woman, and what that meant.

I felt as if I'd been sitting at the Renfros' dinner table. I'd never met anyone quite like these people, and right away I wanted to know more about them.

Nicholson says introducing the Renfros to people who'd never meet them any other way is part of what motivated him to write the story. "The best thing anyone has said about 'Among the Righteous' was a comment made by an artist friend, who said it made her wish she had gone out and taken pictures of some of the old buildings in Washington before they tore them down. I knew what she meant, because I was trying to recapture something of the spirit of a place that is disappearing and something of the values of people who are dying."

Nicholson's editor, Richard Peabody of *Gargoyle,* says writing about "ordinary" people is harder than it sounds because writers must avoid both clichéd sitcom situations and topics that are hip at the moment. "So much coming out of the city deals with the drugs, the more sordid side of street life," he says, "which is almost cliché itself at this point." He says Nicholson could have chosen to write about the boys and their experiences on the street. "But I think to really examine them as a family, that's hard to do. To get all those different aspects of that family. And I like that. I rarely see that sort of full picture."

Peabody says he had hoped to find a story like "Among the Righteous" in his mailbox. "I wasn't looking for an Archie Bunker kind of story of black family life, but what I was looking for was something that had a sort of moralistic stance. I'm not really big on John Gardner's 'moral fiction' but this story had a message and it had something I thought was sort of positive about it, and that hooked me."

Nicholson says the story is based on a tale he'd heard in his family since childhood. At the beginning of the Depression, his grandfather was fired from a janitorial job and came home to tell his wife that they might lose the house they'd just bought.

"The way my mother and aunts always told it, my grandmother told him to go back and tell his supervisor that he could not fire him. He did, and they kept the house—I live in it today."

But Nicholson didn't just set down an actual event. He'd never been told what his grandfather said to his grandmother or how he felt about the whole episode. Nicholson had to create all that.

"He was a proud man, and I imagine he did not take it lightly. But he had a sense of responsibility, so that I imagine that even if, unlike Odis, he went back the next day, it was not an easy thing to do."

Nicholson, who says he's "done all the things writers are supposed to have done: flunked out of college, ridden across the country on Greyhound buses more times than I care to remember, dug ditches, washed dishes, been a reporter and rewrite man," began "Among the Righteous" shortly after graduating from the University of Iowa Writers Workshop. In a class taught by Paule Marshall, he learned how Flannery O'Connor's stories often contain the entire story—or the genesis thereof—in the first paragraph. He also studied with James Alan McPherson, a writer he'd admired since reading his first collection of stories, *Hue and Cry*.

"I set out, then, to try to write a story using what I had gleaned from studying some of my favorite stories by McPherson, and to try to do what Flannery O'Connor did—to set everything up in the first paragraph. I failed, primarily because I think I am a novelist at heart," he says.

Although Nicholson says he failed, take another look at his first paragraph. All the important elements except one—Odis's relationship with his sons—are established there, without the paragraph seeming heavy-handed.

Nicholson worked on the story intermittently over a three-year period, experimenting with past tense and points of view, editing and rewriting. "I took out, for example, a whole section where Wallace and Wilson meet Night Train on the street. Eventually, I came up with two drafts that I cut and pasted together."

At the same time, Nicholson was working on three novels, so he didn't pay much attention to selling the story. But Peabody, who'd read Nicholson's work when sitting on a grants panel for the District of Columbia Commission for the Arts, asked him to submit to *Gargoyle*. By that time, one of the novels had been rejected a few times and he had gotten mired down in another one, so he sent Peabody the story and the opening chapters of two of the novels.

Peabody chose the story. "I really liked the voices in this one," he says. "I think he has a knack for dialogue, a good ear. And then the character of Odis Renfro. I liked him—I just, frankly, quite liked him."

Peabody did little editing, except to point out a few places where lines were repetitive. Only after the story was published did Nicholson notice one discrepancy. In the original story, Daisy refers to having been married twenty years, but Odis had worked for Speidell just seventeen years and was single when he first started. For publication here, Nicholson changed the reference so the math works out.

After the story appeared, Nicholson read it once in public and a friend asked to use it in a creative writing class. It was also selected to be included in an anthology of stories by Washington writers.

Looking at the story now, Nicholson says, "Basically, I like the story. I'm a conservative writer—experiments in form and language don't really interest me much at all." He also thinks he succeeded in accomplishing what he set out to do: experiment with the techniques of two writers he admired and write a reply to "some of the black feminists whose writing has been so popular over the last few years and which, while powerful, tells only the woman's side."

And, of course, introducing the Renfros to some new friends.

What Men Love For

W hen I was twelve, my father called on weeknights to convince my mother that he would return safely that weekend and to assure himself that his house was still in order. The phone's ringing always startled my mother from what she was doing—blowing smoke rings through the window screen or, when she was extremely melancholy, cutting her face out of old pictures of herself. The calls sent her swiftly to the bathroom, where she locked the door and gargled. She had returned home that spring after a nervous breakdown, and she believed that each ring meant my father had driven off some mountainside or had abandoned us because she was a manic depressive. Her worst fear was that he was calling from a pay phone somewhere past the Appalachians, to say he was on his way to sunny and golden California.

"Richard," my father said one night. "You keeping the home motor tuned and purring for your old man?" Our weekend hobby was restoring motorcycles. "How's the chrome tank on that Harley coming along? You got the rust spots off yet?"

"Everything's as shiny as a new dime," I said.

"And your mother. You would tell me if something was wrong again?"

"Old Buck's got everything under control," I said. Buck Rogers was my father's childhood hero, and he trusted me when I called myself that. This was the summer of the moon shot; I suspect almost every father wanted his son to be an astronaut.

"You can count on old Buck." My mother picked up the bedroom extension. My father explained to her that when he came home that weekend, we would grill steaks and make ice cream.

"By God, we might even break out the old Satchmo records and some wine, and dance in the kitchen. Have us a cozy little party with the lights turned low."

My father addressed me, on the kitchen extension, now. "Hey, Richard. They called your old man 'Fleet Foot' back in the days when dancing was dancing." There on the kitchen table my mother had carefully aligned the cut-out faces in one row and the pictures in another. And then my father was rambling again, saying that he was up for a promotion, which would mean less traveling. "After Labor Day, I should be home two days a week, plus week-ends. Two or three years of that and who knows?" His dream was to quit traveling through North Carolina, where we lived, and Virginia. He presented my mother with a version of how life would be once he got the right breaks and became the owner of his own hospital-supply company. "I'd be home every night. The business would be shaky at first, but hell, all businesses are. Ours would be a family enterprise that *worked*. We'd all take an interest in it, make decisions together, things like that."

"You can count old Buck in," I said.

"What about now?" my mother asked.

"Labor Day," my father said. "Let me snag that promotion and I'll be home more. Is that too much to ask?"

"I suppose not." My mother hung up her extension. I said the good-byes for us both. I put the faces and the pictures they'd come from into the photograph box, and then I retrieved a sleeping pill from the supply I kept hidden. I went to where my mother lay in bed, gave her one, and turned the fan on low.

"You have to stop doing this," I said.

"It helps when I feel bad." I had a difficult time understanding what had happened to the woman who had once laughed and clapped as I walked around the kitchen on my hands, saying to her, "This is how they walk in China—upside down," the change tumbling from my pockets. She had been glum and anxious since coming back. "Please don't tell," she had said when I first caught her cutting her face from the pictures. She held the photograph to her face, looking at me through an image of herself, eye blinking and peering where her face had been. At the time I was afraid that my father would guess that her nervousness had returned, and that they would take her away again. These secrets from my father held us together.

"Can we do cat's cradle?" she asked. She had folded her robe over a chair beside the bed, and she took the string from its pocket. I sat beside her and played cat's cradle. The twine slipped from her hands to mine and then back, each exchange making a different configuration. As she slipped into sleep, I made Jacob's ladder, weaving a narrow net of string twisted taut between my fingers. We were strings of a fragile ladder, working in collusion with and against each other.

The cool portion of each morning, I set up a ladder before the dew had evaporated, when no one was stirring on our street except the milkman and husbands taking out the garbage before leaving for work. My job was to reglaze a third-floor window. I learned the simple but universal law that craftsmen somehow know—that working with your hands is a pleasure, especially work so mindless that everything you need to forget becomes absorbed by the sash to be mended. This law's implication is that in routing out a bad strip of glazing, in sanding the sash carefully, protecting the glass pane from the paper's grains with a fingertip, in the decisions made on each of the window's sixteen panes, something small is set straight that affects the universe. Window glazing requires a dangerous angling of your body if the putty lines are to be drawn straight and true. Everything sits arranged on the sill—hammer, sandpaper, primer, points, and putty. The dissonant parts of yourself hang divided in the graph made by the window sash. To fall inward toward your reflection would be as disastrous as falling backward, to the ground. This tension feels natural, good. The morning smelled of sweat and of the linseed oil rubbed into the wood yesterday to revive its vigor. Vigor is also in the worker. Women sense this, and they are pleased.

"I made you some coffee," my mother said one morning. She stood at the ladder's bottom in her robe and slippers. I came down the ladder for the coffee.

"It's going to be a *good* day, isn't it?" A good day meant she would not need crying or the pictures.

"It's going to be a *great* day," I said.

We shared a cigarette. She allowed me to smoke on certain mornings like these. Often she talked to me about the way she felt.

"The problem, Richard, is that everything makes me so sad. It's like Christmas, with all those presents. Most people look at the gifts and think of all the nice things inside. But ever since I was a small girl, I've worried about tearing the wrappers open and finding something inside I didn't want. The wrappers were so pretty, but I was always afraid they were hiding something awful. Is is like that for you? Are you afraid of finding something inside that you don't want?"

I told her that almost anything but long underwear suited me just fine.

"You're like your father. You're lucky you're easy to please. Any other man would probably have left me, I know. I get mad at him for *not* leaving, Richard. Then I get mad when he isn't here. Isn't it strange, the way you feel sometimes?"

"It'll be a good day," I said. "Don't worry."

My mother went inside, and I stood for a moment admiring my work and the sun held tightly in the window. The ladder sagged as I climbed back up. As I passed my mother's room, I stopped to watch her in her bathroom before the mirror. She was brushing her hair, and I was startled when her hair held static and a few strands reached up to grab at the brush. She stroked, stopped to scrutinize something in her face, resumed. The awkwardness of being outside and not able to affect her settled in my stomach. She saw me for an instant and waved and went back to her reflection. The wave was one of those waves you see from someone on a porch when he suddenly notices a passing car and gives in to the urge to establish some kind of human contact.

Saturday afternoons my father said things like "See how this chain fits itself into the teeth of the sprocket?" Home from a week's traveling, he tinkered with motorcycles until dusk. He wore khakis and a sleeveless T-shirt. He bought the motorcycles secondhand—usually from someone who had taken a spill—and restored them. When he had renovated one to mint condition, he sold it, and we began renovating another. Frames hung from the garage's rafters like carcasses. When we got a motorcycle whose rider had been killed, we salvaged the parts. My father wouldn't rebuild those particular motorcycles, nor would he sell to a man with a family. He thought motorcycles were too dangerous for any family man besides himself. His favorite customers were men who had just enlisted. He would tell them to be very careful driving to Fort Bragg and would often talk to them about his own service days. He had been a Navy man, had almost re-enlisted. Before he closed each deal, he gave the buyer a list of maintenance tips and tune-up instructions that he made him promise to follow.

"And what about you?" one of them asked. "You still ride?" We had just sold a Triumph to a recruit. When the man toyed with the clutch, the machine jerked forward in a spasm.

"No. I don't really ride anymore." My father pointed at me and the house where my mother was emerging with tea. "I can't afford the chance of taking a spill." He considered our midnight rides not really riding but something else entirely.

My mother brought us tea in Mason jars; the man wobbled down the driveway and missed second gear. My parents had argued that morning over the promotion my father was to get after Labor Day. She had said that two months was a long time to wait for someone in her condition.

"Condition?" he had asked.

"I missed my period," she had said.

"Here comes the new mother now," my father said. "Here." He helped her with the tray. He said that she should be careful carrying things, especially with two strong men around who could do things for her. All morning she had basked in my father's unexpected attention. My father set down the tea and cornered her and gave her a hug and a nip at her ear.

"Baby money." He presented her with a wad of cash. "What say I get some fat porterhouses and a bottle of wine. French stuff."

"This isn't a substitute for your being here, you know." Then she seemed to understand that she had spoiled the moment, and she rushed back inside the house.

"Pregnant women," my father said. He gave me a wink.

"Should I put some potatoes on?" my mother called.

"The biggest you've got," my father yelled. He looked down the driveway at something the recruit had dropped. My father went and picked up his handwritten instructions.

"He'll probably forget to put oil in the crankcase, and seize it up," he said as we walked to the back yard. My father poured charcoal briquettes into the grill, and I stacked them into a pyramid. "Stand back," he said, and after dousing the charcoal with lighter fluid, he lit the fire. Leaning against the sides of the garage and the fence, scattered like giant cicada husks, were more motorcycles that my father's hands would set into motion. My father got a sad pleasure from selling mint-condition motorcycles to people who, he feared, would ruin them.

Late one Saturday night we stretched out on a blanket in the back yard. My mother sat at the blanket's edge and swayed to the music playing loudly in the kitchen. Louis Armstrong was ejecting lonesome notes from his horn. A box of light spilled out the door and held a portion of my mother. My father pointed out the constellations and gave them names.

"How about a dance?" he said, and gathered my mother up into his arms. When he dipped her, she giggled and hugged the back of his neck. They were two shadows, keeping cadence to Armstrong's melody. Now and then my father stopped and looked up into the night sky. "We could travel to China, Richard, with that night sky and a little luck." They resumed their sleepy dance, and I thought, if you dug down past the roots and the fossils and the dead, you'd hit another world. The idea that our disturbances were a small part of something as immense as the world was dizzying. Men had walked in space a few years before, floating dangerously out to rope's length and then hauling themselves back, their feet searching for firm footing and balance in a realm where none could be found. This was how we were that summer.

"Do my back and shoulders," my mother said. She had tired of dancing, and she sat where the light verged into shadows and darkness. My father loosened her blouse's top button. He kneaded her muscles and called her his "girl." She rubbed and stretched herself against his hands. Soon she fell asleep, and he carried her up the steps. "How about a ride?" he whispered to me as he stepped inside. When he came back out, he stood in the box of light and stretched. Now he said to me again, "How about a ride?" We pushed his Harley to the driveway's edge, so as not to awaken her. The Harley grumbled and came to life with a kick.

My father coaxed the engine gently through the gears. We slid through the night like a snake through slick growth. My father eased into the turns with a knowing motion. He said once that you never really ride a motorcycle; instead you let it take you where it wants to go. We traveled for several hours, retracing the same tired path. We rode until the darkness eased into a notion that dawn would come. That night we circled wide of our sorrows.

"Here we go, Buck." The home stretch of a quarter of a mile was straight and streetlighted. My father turned off the headlight.

To ride a motorcycle at night is a simple thing; you become one with the darkness. The engine's motion works up through your crotch and settles in your chest. You feel caught up in the exhilaration of blind motion. I wore no helmet, and I had conversations with my father that occurred only in my mind.

I warned my father that my mother was doing the best she could but that he might lose her if he was not careful. I explained that people are different from motorcycles; you can't make them into what you want. I felt giddy being a father to my father. I assured him that we were all doing the best we could. I couldn't tell my father what I had learned that summer—that trying might not be enough. I understood that for a long time my mother had suspected this—that trying might not be enough—and had it been in her power to do so, she would have protected me from this sad knowledge. Instead I told him the biggest thing I knew— that my mother, by being at home safe and sleeping, was somehow giving me shelter from the sadness of motorcycles on a summer night. The two of us rushed into the road ahead like two sleepers riding the back of a dream.

"Hell, let's just ride to China," my father always said at our driveway. He slapped his pants pocket, claiming that with his change and a few bills we could make it. He was very proud of his motorcycle's gas mileage. "We *could* get there." *There* covered all the possibilities of where we might be headed.

Sunday morning I often joined my parents in their room. My father snored while my mother read romances. Reading comforted her in much the same way that blowing smoke rings at the screen seemed to comfort her. She was trying to hold things together, warding off depression by intoxicating herself with books whose endings were not surprises. She read romance after romance, all of whose covers pictured forlorn women about to be saved by gentlemen striding confidently out of the background. As she read to me, I watched my father sleep, wondering if she were somehow interpreting his dreams. When he awoke, he scratched his chest and propped himself on a pillow while she gave us a synopsis of this or that book.

"This promising and beautiful young woman is engaged to a doctor. She really loves a poor but honest young butler. He is a servant in the aging doctor's household. It turns out the young butler is the only living heir to a diamond fortune. Mr. Chadworth, a trusted aide to the dying diamond magnate, is commanded to find the last living heir. He successfully locates the butler. She and the butler marry and have a happy life."

"Sounds nice," my father said. "I like to hear you tell us stories." He was up and choosing clothes for his suitcase. "Too bad things are often different."

"Too bad, isn't it." I heard an edge in my mother's voice.

During the week, my mother left the house only at night. We took her car after dark and bought groceries at a grocery store open until ten. My mother drove with the window up, though the air conditioner was broken. She stopped at each intersection and then proceeded in screeching spurts. Once past an intersection, she drove slowly, to avoid any possibility of an accident.

We talked on these rides to the store, my mother usually fretting over my father's absence.

"Just let him get his promotion," I said.

"I'm not worried," my mother said. "Another baby will make him stay at home, I bet."

I said it probably would.

"Do I ruin things when he's at home?"

"Not that I know of."

"It's been a good few weeks, hasn't it?"

"Very good," I said.

"It's too early for me to start showing. You understand that, don't you?"

Another time, she said, "I hear you on that motorcycle late Saturday nights. Whatever on earth do you do?"

"We just ride."

"Just ride?"

"Yeah. It's like all of us being on the bed when you tell a story. It's like early morning when we share a cigarette while I'm glazing."

The last Saturday of that month, while my mother visited her psychiatrist, my father and I hunted arrowheads. We took his Harley out to a field with a stone outcropping where the Indians had gotten flint for arrowheads. We parked the motorcycle beside a road sign that warned of low-flying airplanes. A mile away an airstrip for crop dusters had been cut from the tobacco fields and a tract of pine. The planes took off slowly and wobbled in low over the fields of tobacco, spraying them and then floating straight upward where the field gave way to the pines. We were far enough away for a lag to occur between the sight of the plane's rising and the sound of the pilot's gunning the motor. In the far distance cars on the interstate we had exited moved at a sleepy speed. My father and I spread out through the field and poked at the earth's raw redness. It had rained that morning, and humidity made the air seem as heavy as the mud on my shoes. We made several passes through the field, our paths slowly coiling to its center. When airplane shadows passed over me, I had the urge to run catch them and jump on them like a magic carpet. My father and I always met under a pine tree left for shade in the years when the field was planted with tobacco and the workers needed a spot to rest from the sun.

My father got excited when he found an unfinished arrowhead. "This old boy sure knew what he was doing." He showed me a tip with one side left unfinished.

"I think we can do it better," he said. He took out his pocket knife with the bone handle. He began pressure-flaking at what some Indian had abandoned three centuries earlier. My father squatted on his hams. His veins grew into a web as he tried to remove the flakes in exactly the right places. Now and then he struck the arrowhead a quick tap. Earlier that morning he had argued with my mother, accusing her of blaming him for things that were beyond his control. My father's knife *tick-tick-ticked,* and he seemed a child again, fumbling to make something whose exact shape he was still trying to discover.

Instead of a promotion they gave my father responsibility for half the state of Tennessee. This meant he would be gone even more. The whole Saturday morning of Labor Day weekend he refused to talk. Instead he cleaned and recleaned his Harley's spark plugs. Then he readjusted their gap. He cranked the engine again and again, listening to the cylinders' compression. Then he attached the plugs and laid them against the casing. He kicked the starter to watch their arc.

"It's my fault," my mother said. She came out from the bedroom to stand behind me where I stood at the kitchen door, watching. She had the box of photographs under her arm and a note in her hand. She told me to give the note to my father. Then she locked herself in the bedroom.

I read the note and then carried it to my father. The note

said, "You've been doubting that you love me for some time now. If it's another mouth to feed that you're worried about, don't. I just made the baby up."

"Here," I said. He stuck it in his pocket. He had the plugs back in and was working degreaser into his hands.

"You might want to read it now."

He read it and threw down the rag with which he was cleaning away the loosened grease. When I got into the house, he was banging on the bedroom door.

"For God's sake, open up," my father said.

"Just leave," my mother said. "Love me or leave me, but the way things are now has to stop."

"Why did you claim to be *pregnant?* Just to trick me?"

"Didn't you notice how things changed when you thought I was pregnant?"

"Open up right now," my father said. "You hear me? Open up right this minute."

"I'm not coming out until you calm down," my mother said. "I might not even come out until this afternoon." She started slipping the faceless pictures of herself under the door.

"What in the hell is this supposed to mean?" he asked.

"It's how I feel. Have you spent so much time traveling that you can't understand *that?*"

"I understand one thing—it's time for a change. I'm taking my son with me, and I'm going to get drunk. D-R-U-N-K." He led me from the house to the Harley.

My father didn't get drunk that night, but by nightfall we had made the Appalachians. My father stopped at a tourist trap named Blowing Rock. It was near a road tunnel that fed through the mountains into Tennessee. We parked by an information sign that told of the legend of Blowing Rock. An Indian maiden jumped, and her lover, returning late from the hunt, saw her fall. He prayed so hard as she tumbled in the wind that God heard, and He blew her back up to the cliff's edge and safety.

"What the hell," my father said. "An Indian Lover's Leap." The sign said that this legend explained why anything thrown off

Blowing Rock rose back up. On a windy day it could snow *upward* here.

My father stood near the guardrail and scratched his head. He pulled a cigar from his jacket and licked and puffed at it. He held himself to three a week. "This is the best way to taste a cigar," he said, and I didn't know if he would light it. Finally he did.

"Sometimes I believe she does everything in her power to drive me away. Richard, I never bargained for a crazy woman, even if I *do* love her. The hell of it is, I never once thought it would turn out this way." The cigar glowed and blinked at intervals. "There goes my own business," he said. "Tennessee." He pointed toward the darkness where the mountains, though invisible, could be felt.

"It's not like you've really been home a lot," I said.

"Well, they sure fixed that problem for me, didn't they. I can't work for them after they throw me stinking Tennessee." He looked at me with bewilderment. "Richard, what if your mother and I *can't* make a go of it?"

My father reached into his pockets and gathered his change. With his head making an arc of light, he motioned me to follow. "Let's try this out, Buck." He leaned over the guardrail. He pitched coin after coin off the mountain's edge, leaning as far as he could to watch where they went. We felt no wind that night, and of course they did not rise. After the coins he tried rocks and sticks and even paper cups rummaged from the trash bin. In the moonless night he was a shadow gathering pieces and tossing them off. Each object was sucked from sight as it fell. He stood there, a man tossing things off a mountainside, caught in the human hope that they would rise again as promised. The night was as dark as I imagined the far side of the moon might be. The thought occurred to me that though we could, we wouldn't keep going west; we had gone as far as it was possible to go and still turn back.

My father crushed the cigar near the motorcycle. "Climb aboard, Buck." We drove to the main highway and turned toward home. I thought of how the road leading down from the mountainside was steep and dangerous. Around one bend or another would lie a blind curve whose far side held secret what might or might not be. As we approached that curve there would arise in us a steady drumming. Our chests would swell and throb until our pulse beat in the quicks of our fingertips. We were blood-full of the moment wherein, against all probabilities, you lean into the curve and take your chances of making it. You feel earthbound, not by the motorcycle but by your urge to round that bend. Oil slick or happy ending, complete with a hero's welcome, you ease into that snake of road whose other side holds your future hidden. This moment is what men love for. You are father and son, caught in a homeward motion.

"Hold on," my father said, and we went at that curve with all the speed and hope that we could muster.

Notes

The idea for "What Men Love For" came to Dale Ray Phillips while he was fishing. "I remember thinking that the idea was worth worrying over, and I remember catching my limit that day," he says.

When he got home he wrote a rough draft, then put it aside for a while. He reworked that draft a couple of times, eliminating a grandmother he had in the story, at one point, to tighten it up. He sent the story out twice, and it was rejected twice.

"I thought, 'I can't write any better than this right now.' I got a little frustrated but I just kept sending it back out." He had a list of publications posted on the wall and tried to get the story out to the next magazine of the list the same day it came back. "I believed the story would eventually go somewhere, I just didn't know where," he says.

Writers have to remain philosophical, Phillips says. "You've got to treat a rejection slip like an acceptance slip—go out and have a beer."

The philosophy paid off when C. Michael Curtis, senior editor at the *Atlantic Monthly,* called to say he wanted the story.

Phillips has "a good ear for the way people talk and feel and a sense of how the vicissitudes of life lead us to hard decisions and sometimes to sad choices," Curtis says. He sees the story as a somewhat sentimental tale about "the special relationship that can develop between a father and a son and the way each, through some dim understanding of what matters most to the other, can reach out to the other."

Curtis didn't edit the story heavily. He recommended that Phillips change the model of motorcycle from BMW to Harley-Davidson because most people think of cars when they hear BMW.

A researcher at the *Atlantic* also called Phillips to say that one of the father's maintenance tips wasn't correct. The father said of a customer, "He'll probably forget to put oil in the crankcase, and bust the block." The researcher had called several motorcycle repair shops and said forgetting to put oil in the crankcase wouldn't bust the block, but would seize it up. Phillips approved the change.

"They changed a few little glitches like that and cleaned some of my sentences up, but there were no major scene rewrites at all," Phillips says.

Curtis says that kind of editing is common at his magazine. "We take care of small details that a lot of writers don't have the patience or interest to attend to and as a consequence the stories, when they finally are published, have been examined with great care and great precision."

One aspect that concerned Phillips when he submitted the story wasn't changed.

"I was a little worried about the title," he says. "I was prepared to change it to something like 'Why Men Love' because 'What Men Love For' is grammatically incorrect. I was afraid someone would look at that and say, 'I'm not going to read this. The guy can't even get a title straight.'"

But he went with the title despite his reservations. "It was the only way I could figure out to get in the notion that that one moment is both the *object* of their love and the *reason* for their love."

Curtis didn't see any problem with the title. "We liked the sound of it and it seemed appropriate to the story, so we saw no reason to change it," he says. "We ordinarily like to stay with the titles authors give their stories unless we think they're awkward or misconceived, in which case we will suggest alternatives."

While they both talked about the story with surety, neither Phillips or Curtis was inclined to discuss it in much detail. "Writers probably should write, not talk," Phillips said simply. Curtis said he likes stories because he responds to them on a visceral level and "to try to pull the stories apart as an academic critic is not my mode."

Even so, the story stands up to close examination. Both Phillips and Curtis touched on the ambiguity that's reflected in the title. At first it's hard to be sure if the author is trying to tell you something about *why* men love or *what* they love. But by the final scene it becomes clear he means both: "We were blood-full of the moment wherein, against all probabilities, you lean into the curve and take your chances of making it. . . . This moment is what men love for." Richard and his father both love that moment—it is, as Phillips said,

the object of their love. And because they share the love of that moment—as Curtis put it, they understand what matters most to each
other—they are able to reach out to each other.

That final moment is the culmination of the title's promise, but
the story is full of such moments—moments that define Richard's relationship with his parents and him as an individual.

There is the moment when Richard first finds his mother cutting
her face out of pictures and begins sharing her secret. There is the
moment at the ladder, when she allows him a cigarette and talks
about her fears about pretty packages. Richard is bound to his
mother by secrets—the secrets of the photographs and the cigarettes, and the bigger secret that they had both learned that summer:
that trying might not be enough.

With his father, there are the times spent repairing motorcycles
and riding them in the dark. There is the hunt for arrowheads and his
father's tapping away at the unfinished one. His father, Richard
knows, is trying to fix things, to shape them into some semblance of
the life he expected. So his silent conversation with his father in-
cludes this: "I explained that people are different from motorcycles;
you can't make them into what you want."

And then there are Richard's moments. Working on the ladder,
enjoying the precision of reglazing a window and the tension of balancing between two equally dangerous fates. Passing by his mother's room, facing the knowledge that he couldn't affect her. A boy
becoming a man rather quickly.

What happens? They go on. The mother lies in her bed at night,
allowing Richard and his father to slip off into the darkness time after
time. Richard and his father turn back from their escape to come
home again time after time. They are, all three of them, going at that
snake of road whose other side holds the future hidden with all the
speed and hope they can muster.

The Village

The village was ancient. It lay nestled in a peaceful valley in the Central Highlands, midway between Hanoi and Saigon and just forty kilometers from the South China Sea.

The first houses built upon these same sites had been houses of mud walls mixed with rice-straw binder and thatched rice-straw roofs (as were these houses).

The first time that the village was destroyed in war (it had been destroyed many times before that by flood) was during the War of the Two Villages, or the War Between the North and the South. The village had been destroyed by war many other times by the Chinese, the Cambodians, the Chinese, the Thailanders, the Huns, the Chinese, the French, and the Japanese.

The people of the village had become so good at having their village destroyed by war that they knew exactly how to go about it. First they would hide all the food and plows and scythes. They would drive all the water buffalo into the jungle. Then, gathering all the people of the village except for one old and worthless grandmother who was too weak to travel, they would disappear into the jungle. The village had been destroyed so many times and the people of the village had become so good at having it destroyed that the village actually did not exist any more; in fact it had never existed, and neither had the people who were so good at disappearing. It was all an illusion, but it did not matter because the soldiers who were coming to destroy it and who had always come to destroy it were an illusion also; and all the wars, and all their causes that had ever destroyed the village were also illusions. In fact everything was an illusion except for the jungle, which was an orderly place where things existed to be killed and eaten. All humankind and all the possessions and passions of humankind

JIM PITZEN

· ·

123

(including war) were illusions. Human beings had created themselves in their own minds (they were fabrications of their own imaginations) and their minds were such disorderly places that they had forgotten how or why they had created themselves so they were doomed to wander about trying to uncreate themselves.

The jungle and the mosquitoes and the leeches were orderly because they had not been created but had always been and always would be, and they fit in their natural place and knew it and did not try to be anything else. The jungle and the mosquitoes and the leeches watched with amusement the imaginary soldiers destroying the illusory village over and over and over again, and they sucked the imaginary blood of the imaginary soldiers just to keep up the illusion.

"Cheechee, cheechee," the monkey called.

The slightly built, blond soldier jumped awake, at first frightened, then guilty. He'd been sleeping on guard again. At dawn, too, the worst time. He squirmed around. The soaked jungle fatigues had given him a swimming-suit itch all over except on his bare brown arms where the mosquitoes feasted. He wiped them off, killing fifteen or twenty on each arm.

Fucking mosquitoes, he thought, fucking monsoon. The mosquitoes buzzed and the rain dripped from the huge-leafed banana tree above him. His jungle boot reached out and nudged Hardje's foot.

Hardje awoke instantly. His thumb checked the safety on his M-16. He wiped the mosquitoes from his bare brown arms. He whispered, "What?"

Tyler whispered back, "Almost dawn."

Hardje sat up, shivered; his wet jungle fatigues clung to him.

Light began to grow in the east and spread slowly. Tyler whispered, "You need a shave."

"So fucking what," Hardje said.

They sat and listened to the elephant grass grow; green, six feet tall, taller, and still growing. The rain hissed. Monkeys called. Parrots began to quarrel.

Hardje grunted and said, "They're not going to hit us. They'd of done it by now."

Tyler wiped at the mosquitoes and nodded. "Listen to the parrots."

Hardje wiped the mosquitoes from his arms and stood up slowly, groaning at the stiffness in his muscles. "Son of a bitch," he said.

Tyler grinned and said, "I fell asleep again. Just at dawn. Dammit. I can't stay awake at dawn."

Hardje shrugged. "Neither can anyone else."

The parrots and monkeys called.

Hardje started to wipe the mosquitoes from his arm, changed his mind, and scratched his neck instead. He said, "Well, leech time."

He pulled down his pants (nobody wore underwear anymore because of jock itch) and removed his shirt. His rear end and legs glowed white next to his mahogany arms and chest and back. The leeches, black and two inches long, clung to him, one on each inner thigh, two more at the beltline, one on his back just beneath the shoulder blade. Red pockmarks scattered over his skin traced the leeches that had gone before.

"Mosquito dope?" Tyler asked.

The mosquito dope, G.I. Gin, made the leeches curl up, writhing, and let go, but the alcohol made the bites burn like fire.

"Fuck it," Hardje answered. He began slowly pulling off a leech, one of the two at his beltline. The reddened, irritated skin lifted with the leech, its suction-cup mouth clinging. Then the leech let go suddenly. Bright blood trickled down Hardje's lower stomach and disappeared into the reddish-brown pubic hair. He threw the leech down and stamped it into the ground.

"Fucking things," Hardje said. "Fucking valley."

With a steady hand he pulled off three more leeches, tossing them into the tall grass. "How in hell do they get in your pants?" he said. "I had my pants tucked into my boots, and my belt was so fucking tight I couldn't breathe."

Tyler shrugged and wiped the mosquitoes from his arms.

Hardje looked over his shoulder. "Get that bastard, will you?" Tyler stood and pulled the leech from Hardje's back.

"Rain's letting up," Hardje said.

Tyler nodded.

"You leech yourself yet?" Hardje asked.

Tyler shook his head no.

"Talkative bastard, ain't you," Hardje said.

Tyler nodded and began to strip as Hardje started to dress.

The rain had stopped but would continue to fall from the canopy of trees covering them like a tent.

"Sun's gonna shine," Hardje said. "Gonna get hotter than hell."

He took his entrenching tool and scraped the rotting vegetation from a small spot on the ground. As the leaves turned over, an exposed leech curled and uncurled. "Rotten bastard," Hardje said. He ground it into the mud beneath his heel. "It ain't natural. We're half a mile from the river, and these bastards are all over."

Tyler plucked a blood-engorged leech from near his groin and looked around. He impaled the leech on one of the bright green, three-inch-long thorns that covered the trunk of a nearby tree. He grinned as the leech squirmed and bled.

"What are you grinning about?" Hardje said. "It's your blood."

"I only had one," Tyler said. He pulled his pants up, trapping several mosquitoes.

"Of course," Hardje said. "You ain't as sweet as I am."

Tyler dug into a side pocket of his backpack and retrieved an empty C-ration can with holes punched in the bottom. He set it on the small patch of ground Hardje had cleared. He reached into another pocket of his backpack and brought out a small wad of C.4, a plastic explosive for blowing bunkers and tunnels. He rolled it into a tight wad the size of a walnut and dropped it into the C-ration-can stove. He opened a can of beans and franks almost all the way around with his P-38 can opener, pried the lid back, and, using it as a handle, set the can carefully on the stove.

He pulled a plastic bag from his shirt pocket, unrolled it, and took out a book of matches. The C.4 flared wildly and burned out in five seconds; the beans and franks bubbled. Tyler lifted the can off the stove, sat down on the wet ground, and began eating with a plastic spoon. He watched Hardje open a can of ham and lima beans and shuddered as he set them on the stove.

"You ever seen wood ticks?" he asked Hardje.

Hardje nodded. "I'm from Minnesota."

"Lima beans look like big gray wood ticks on a dog's neck."

Hardje grinned. "Next time you get a can of wood ticks, give 'em to me. I'll eat 'em." He took a big bite, chewed, swallowed, and belched.

Tyler shook his head sadly and said, "No couth. That's your problem. You ain't got no couth."

Swenson, coming up from the next position to the south, parted the elephant grass. "Saddle up," he said. "We're moving out in fifteen. Pass the word."

He turned and disappeared as Hardje began to move toward Cadwell's position to the north. Tyler chopped a hole in the ground and threw the empty cans in it. He put away his stove and lit a Camel, sitting down alongside his pack. He wiped the mosquitoes from his arms. The thin material of his jungle fatigues was already dry except for the seat of the pants and the spots where the trees had dripped. He couldn't see the sun but knew it must be out. Steam was rising from the ground in pillars. He flicked the ember from his cigarette, sliced the paper with his thumbnail, scattered the tobacco, and rolled the paper into a tiny ball that he ground beneath his heel. He checked the safety on his M-16, thought about another cigarette, changed his mind, and sat.

Hardje appeared out of the steam, his uniform soaked from the wet grass. He dropped to one knee, wiped the mosquitoes from his arms, and said, "Guess who got point?"

Tyler stared at him in disbelief. "Christ. You just had it last week."

Hardje nodded and sat down. They sat not talking. Finally Tyler said, "Bastards."

Hardje nodded again. They sat. Swenson shouted, "Everyone pull back to the trail."

The trail was not on any map. It was, possibly, just a game trail, but it wandered more or less in the right direction, following the monsoon-swollen river, crossing and recrossing it, down out of the highlands toward the east and the An Loa Valley twenty kilometers away, toward the South China Sea.

The yellow clay floor of the trail was slippery and sticky. The clay built up on the cleats of Hardje's canvas jungle boots, making him three inches taller. With every step, his feet slid and skidded. The sweat poured out. He wiped the mosquitoes off his arms and checked the safety on his M-16.

Point position. The first man in the company. The lead man. The first man to hit the shit. Point position. Life-expectancy: three days.

Hardje moved slowly down the trail. The jungle was quiet. He watched the ground, the trail, the trees. Watched for trip wires, slender threads attached to booby-trapped mortar rounds, to grenades. Watched for punji stakes, splinters of bamboo smeared in human feces, guaranteed infection if one scratched your skin. Watched for snipers who tied themselves to the tree tops. Watched for ambush. Watched for pit vipers, for cobras. Watched. Sweat burned his eyes. His stomach felt tight, wanted to vomit. The trail wound through the jungle. Hardje stopped, looked back, caught Swenson's attention. He pointed at the punji stakes hidden in the tall grass. Swenson nodded. Hardje wiped the mosquitoes from his arms, moved on. Up a slight rise, then down to the yellow river that tore at its banks. He hesitated, watched the other bank, sick with fear. A perfect ambush spot. He watched, sweat burning his eyes. He checked the safety on his M-16 and plunged into the water. Waist-high water deepened to his armpits near the tall, curved bank on the far side. Then he was across, scrambling up the slippery bank, holding his breath, into the jungle. Nothing. No Charlie. He went back to the bank and waved the company across.

Hardje moved down the trail and sat on a rotting log. The training manual said that an infantry company should be able to march four miles an hour. It had taken him half an hour to go half a mile, yet he felt that he was moving too fast.

The company gathered on the trail behind him. He saw Tyler and waved. The company commander signaled him to move out. He groaned and cursed under his breath but stood up and began the cautious movement once more, watching.

Tyler wiped the mosquitoes from his arms and watched Hardje move out of sight around a bend in the trail. Tyler felt guilty that he wasn't on point. It had been three weeks. He also felt angry about his guilt. He knew Hardje was the best point man in the company. But still, it was past his turn. On and on the argument went as he moved with the company.

The saturated ground steamed in the 120-degree heat. This week's marching song, the song Tyler used to blot out all thought, started to run through his mind. "When Johnnie Comes Marching Home Again." Last week it had been "Up, Up and Away."

The company moved down the trail, one hundred men, eighteen to twenty years old, one hundred thousand thoughts about dying and being paralyzed and having arms and legs blown away and being bitten by snakes and spiders and centipedes and being stung by scorpions. Thinking of people back home. Thinking how glad they were that Hardje was on point. One hundred men with sweat-soaked uniforms, with huge backpacks that occasionally clinked and clunked.

Hardje paused to watch a dark purple butterfly on a black flower, and the company slowed and stopped behind him. He moved on down the trail and they followed.

Hardje paused as a mottled green and yellow, eighteen-foot constrictor slithered across the trail. He grinned as he thought about Tyler's snake phobia. He'd tell Tyler about this one tonight. He wiped the mosquitoes from his arms. Sweat washed the blood away. He checked the safety on his M-16 and moved on. The company followed.

The steaming trail dropped abruptly back down to another river crossing. Hardje stopped, checked his watch. Ten o'clock. He remembered a deer-hunting trip in the snow, how the buck's bloody entrails steamed as he plunged his stinging hands in the body cavity to remove them. He stared at the opposite bank. Stared. Sliding down the bank into the river, up to his waist, to his armpits, then across and scrambling up the other bank and back into the jungle. The company followed, cursing and grumbling and clinking and clanking.

Down the yellow trail. A trail that grew wider as other foot trails joined it from the hills (or took off from it into the hills). Hardje knew these small trails meant that Charlie used the path for disbursing the weapons and food that came in by sea. He moved down the trail watching each step, watching ahead. He stopped on the edge of a small clearing. Rice paddies and dikes, half a mile across, and on the far side, a small village. He signaled for the company to halt, watched as the company commander worked his way through the men who had collapsed alongside the trail. Hardje wiped the mosquitoes from his arms. He saw a huge, hairy tarantula the size of his hand walk across the trail, lifting high two or three legs at a time and planting them carefully, as if it didn't like the mud. Hardje shuddered.

The C.O. said from ten feet away, "What's up, Norway?"

Hardje pointed with his chin.

The C.O. looked around the rice paddy, at the village. He cursed softly. "Son of a bitch. This isn't on the map. How many houses?"

Hardje replied, "Fifteen. Maybe more."

The C.O. nodded. "Well, move out to the first dike and wait for the company to catch up. We'll have to search and destroy the vil. I'll try and get battalion headquarters on the horn."

Hardje waded up to his waist in the shitty-smelling water. He fingered the safety of his M-16, crouched, and waded toward the dike. He heard the company entering the water behind him but kept his eyes glued on the houses and the trees, expecting to die at any time. When the men all reached the dike and crouched down, the word came down the line: "Take it."

As one man, the company rose, clambered over the dike, slid into the next lower paddy, waded, and clambered over the next dike, slid into the next lower rice paddy, and waded.

Hardje and Tyler flicked the safeties off their M-16s and leaped into the first house and halfway across the dirt floor. They stood, holding their breath. Nothing happened. Quiet. There were only two more rooms. Two black, open doorways. They stood staring, waiting for the other to choose a door. Then from the door on the left came the most unearthly wail that either man had ever heard. Their knees sagged. They wanted to vomit, to run, but hadn't the strength to do either. They looked at each other and, rifles ready, entered the room.

When their eyes adjusted to the dark, they saw on a bed of rice-straw mats an incredibly old woman. (They couldn't tell if she was man, woman, or monkey, but they somehow knew.)

She was not much larger than a two-year-old child, shriveled, shrunken, sightless, toothless, nearly hairless, her feet and hands curled up like claws. As they stood, staring, she once again emitted the hideous, shrieking moan. Tyler turned to run but Hardje grabbed him, steadied him. They stared at each other, at her.

The two men stretched Hardje's poncho out alongside the old woman, slid her onto it, and carried her out of the cryptlike blackness of the room, through the main room of the house and into the sunlight. They called for a medic and told the radio operator to call in a Med-Evac chopper because the woman was in pain.

Actually she had been moaning not in pain but because the other people who did not live in the village and who did not disappear when the soldiers did not come out of the jungle had taken from her finger the brass ring that had belonged to her great-great-great-grandmother. The people who did not disappear took the ring because they felt that the soldiers who were not coming to the village that wasn't there would think it was gold and would steal it. So the grandmother was really moaning about her missing ring, and she never moaned again because she died when the sunlight hit her, though the men in the company never knew it because the medic refused even to look at her because she was so ugly. They loaded the old woman on the helicopter and she was never again seen in the village by the people who didn't live there nor by the nonexistent soldiers.

The knot of men watched the chopper pound away toward the south and Landing Zone Linda. The C.O. said, "All right, break it up. One grenade would get you all. Let's finish searching the vil. When you're done we'll burn what will burn and blow the walls with C.4."

The men carried all military-looking items to the hard-packed yard of the house that had been cleared by Hardje and Tyler. The most dangerous-looking items were a crossbow; an old curve-bladed sword; a long-barreled French muzzle-loader; and a small bronze statue of a gargoyle-faced dog with a dragon's tail, which had a star at the end.

Tyler leaned back in the shade of a coconut palm. He checked the safety on his M-16 and laid it across his lap. He opened a can of C-ration beef stew. Hardje wiped the mosquitoes from his arms and leaned back against the wall of the house and began eating his canned scrambled eggs, white bread, and peanut butter.

Each man swallowed a pink salt tablet, a large orange malaria tablet, and a small white malaria tablet and began to eat, more with resignation than with relish.

"I hate this shit," Hardje said conversationally.

Tyler shrugged. "It doesn't matter," he said. He belched. He looked to the west, at the bank of clouds that was crowding the mountains. "Be raining in an hour. This place'll never burn. We'll have to blow it all."

Hardje nodded. He finished the cold eggs and tossed the can over his shoulder, through the glassless window and into the house, where it clunked across the hard floor. Hardje lit a cigarette with a Zippo lighter, sighed. "Well," he said, "I suppose we might as well start."

Tyler nodded and pitched his garbage after Hardje's. He lit a cigarette and stood up. Grabbing his entrenching tool from his pack, he stepped to the house and began chopping the soil away from the foundation. When he judged the area was large enough, he packed C.4 against the foundation, stuck a blasting cap in it, and packed the mud back around the C.4. He strung electrical wire, which was connected to the blasting cap, over to the front yard where the others were waiting with other wires. Hardje wired them all to one main wire and began wading across the rice paddy to the closest dike, unrolling wire as he went.

When all the charges were set and all the wires strung and all the men down behind the rice paddy dike, the C.O. ordered, "Fire the hole!"

Hardje turned back once to look at the village. The cloud of dust still hung in the air. Just then, as if someone had turned on a switch, the rain started again and Hardje turned and plunged once more down the trail, under the dark canopy of leaves, looking carefully for booby traps and snipers and ambushes, and the company behind him followed with clinking, clunking packs.

Down the muddy trail under the dripping trees. Measuring time not in hours or minutes but in aching, weary steps. Shoulders slumping beneath the straps of heavy packs. Step by step, one step at a time, pick up a heavy foot and swing it forward, slog it down into the mud, a few thousand steps and a mile and a few muddy miles and a few more muddy miles and it was nearly dark and the C.O. signaled to set up a perimeter.

Hardje and Tyler readied their position without a word. Hardje chopped the tall grass, clearing firing lanes. Tyler set out trip flares and Claymore mines. Tyler pulled his stove from his pack and asked Hardje if he had any C.4 left. Hardje, standing in the gathering darkness, wiped the mosquitoes from his arms and nodded. "In the side pocket," he said.

As Tyler reached for the pack, his hand brushed Hardje's M-16. It tipped, falling. Tyler grabbed for it. His finger touched the trigger. Hardje had forgotten to check the safety back in the village

because the old woman had unnerved him. The shell exploded.
Hardje bent over. Looked at Tyler. Sat down.

Tyler said, "No."

He jumped to Hardje's side, asked, "Where?"

He saw Hardje's hands clutching his lower stomach. He un-
buckled Hardje's belt, pulled his pants down, his shirt up. There
was a tiny hole, not much larger than a leech scar. A stream of
blood trickled down and lost itself in reddish-brown pubic hair.

"It doesn't look bad," Tyler said. "It really doesn't."

Hardje's eyes glazed over.

Tyler frantically rolled him over on his stomach. Steaming
red entrails with globs of yellow fat poured out a hole the size of
his fist in the middle of Hardje's back. The blood burned Tyler's
hands as he tried to stuff the guts back in.

Mosquitoes drawn by the blood swarmed.

A leech slowly, sinuously slithered beneath Tyler's belt and
snuggled up in the wet warmth of his groin. Tyler wiped the mosquitoes from his unfeeling arms as he cried.

The people who did not live in the village that wasn't there
heard the steel blades of the phantom helicopter chopping
through the monsoon with Hardje's imaginary corpse. They
looked up and saw its spectral shape slipping through the shadows of the clouds, and they stirred their rice.

Notes

The first time I read "The Village," I was so taken with the opening paragraphs that I read them aloud to a friend. I remember particularly these lines:

The village had been destroyed so many times and the people of the village had become so good at having it destroyed that the village actually did not exist any more; in fact it had never existed, and neither had the people who were so good at disappearing. It was all an illusion, but it did not matter because the soldiers who were coming to destroy it and who had always come to destroy it were an illusion also; and all the wars, and all their causes that had ever destroyed the village were also illusions.

I had read many stories about Vietnam and had struggled to understand the experience that shaped so many of my generation. But here was something new, an insight I hadn't had before. This wonderfully lyrical passage showed me "our" war in a larger perspective—not placed against the personal dramas or the political climate of the times, but against an absurdly hopeless and unbroken cycle of war that changed nothing. The frustration and uselessness overwhelmed me.

Jim Pitzen says that was his experience of Vietnam. "There were times when I felt like it was happening to someone else or not really happening. I had to detach from it that way to live through it. It was that kind of experience for me. There were times when it was just ultrasharp and each instant was an hour long and there were other times that it just seemed like it didn't make any difference. No matter what we did it was just going to be the same. That we weren't making any difference at all—that things were the way they had been and always would be."

Writing about such a personal and painful experience is always difficult. For Pitzen, the story came only after years of trying to cope with the after-effects of a year as an infantryman with the First Cavalry. When he returned from Vietnam in 1967, he began drinking and using drugs. He tried to block out the pain. "It was five years before

I even started having nightmares," he recalls. "I had it that well re-pressed. It took that long for it to start coming out."

After eleven years when he "never drew a sober breath," Pitzen got off the drugs and alcohol and started trying to write a novel. "This stuff started trying to come out, but it was just so *bad*. I knew it was bad, so I quit."

In 1981, he went back to college at Bemidji State College, where he eventually earned a bachelor's in English. While he was there, he started "The Village."

"It was kind of a catharsis. When you no longer have the drugs and alcohol to cover up, you have to do something with that stuff and you have to look at it and deal with the pain. That's part of what that process was."

The story began with an incident that happened in Vietnam, where one friend shot another. "I started writing about the incident and then that part about the village, that kind of surrealistic part, it just started coming out and I just went with the flow, let it go."

At first, the description of the village appeared in the middle of the story, when the soldiers first see the village. But as he worked, Pitzen began to realize that the village was central to the story and moved the description to the beginning. And while he rewrote the rest of the story at least five times (especially the dialogue, which he says was stilted and clumsy), he didn't change those paragraphs much.

When he finished the revisions, he titled the story "One Day in Leech Valley" and sent it to Jay Schaefer, editor of *Fiction Network*. It was the first story he'd ever submitted.

Schaefer didn't know Pitzen had never been published, but he thought the story had something to say and said it clearly and powerfully.

"The writing was very sincere and honest," he recalls. "The au-thor didn't try to do anything particularly fancy. There were no work-shop tricks involved. He hadn't followed a particular formula. The story seemed to flow out of the events and the events seemed very real and very immediate. I don't mean necessarily true—they may or may not have been true, I don't know—but they had a directness and a powerful clarity that rang true."

By luck, the editors at *Fiction Network* were especially interested in good stories about Vietnam. "At that time it was a relatively
new area being explored in fiction. That's what led us to the story
initially."

But Schaefer says that while Pitzen's story was well timed, its
Vietnam theme isn't what got it published. "We don't set out to look
for particular types of stories. We're looking for good writing," he
says.

In this case, the description of the village and Pitzen's sincerity
were the deciding factors. "The way he led into the very dramatic
events with a series of passages that convey the feeling of thousands
of years of the culture of Vietnam and the history of the village was
very effective. Without using a device that seemed self-conscious he
was able to capture the ancientness of the village and the cycle of
life and the cycle of war very efficiently in a very few paragraphs."

Schaefer warns writers that while the history motif works well in
"The Village," it might not work in other cases. "I can't say that *every*
story should have that or every *war* story should have that. . . . Don't
look for formula answers. You have to know what you're writing about.
I don't think anyone doubts the author knew his subject matter here.
He wrote from the heart and had a story to tell. That's essential for
successful stories."

Schaefer did little editing of Pitzen's story. Pitzen says he pointed
out a few redundancies and encouraged him to use "he said" in passages of dialogue, rather than phrases such as "he exclaimed."
"I liked the changes he suggested," Pitzen says.

"What I tried to do was bring out more clearly what the author
already had down on the page," Schaefer says. He doesn't force
changes on authors. "The editing process is really a consensual one.
It's the *author's* story. I see the role of an editor as to bring out what
the author intended, not to write the *editor's* story."

Schaefer did, however, suggest a new title. " 'The Village'
seemed to have much more impact as a title and seemed to be what
the story was about," he says. He suggested that change without
knowing Pitzen had moved the passage about the village to the beginning during rewriting, but it completed the transformation from a

story about a horrible accident in Vietnam into a bigger story about the effects of war. "Really when I thought about it, the story was about the village. It wasn't about a day in Leech Valley," Pitzen says now.

Schaefer says titles often are changed. "Frequently people try and do too much in the title. They try and say too much, or get too clever, or get too subtle. What I look for is a title that is simple and direct and doesn't get in the way, and is also somewhat inviting to the reader. 'One Day in Leech Valley' didn't grab me, didn't make me want to read the story."

After the story was published, it received the O. Henry Prize and was published in *Prize Stories 1987*. Pitzen, who admits he suffers from "chronic low self-esteem" says, "My first thought was, 'Boy, that's wonderful.' My second thought was, 'There must not have been many good stories published.' It didn't seem right that it was happening."

While the attention from the O. Henry award initially made him feel as if his first story were a hard act to follow, he's currently rewriting a novel about a drug-addicted Vietnam veteran who's institutionalized. Rewriting, he says, is crucial. "I've got three or four friends whose instincts in literature I trust and I have them read [a finished piece] because a lot of times I can't see myself objectively enough. I really seriously consider the changes they suggest. I don't always make them, but I always consider them."

He says he learned the importance of rewriting from the poet Michael Dennis Brown, who said, "You must learn to kill your darlings." He advises other writers to follow that advice, as he does. "I'm not afraid to tear a story apart and rewrite it, change everything around."

The secret of rewriting, of course, is to recognize what's good and throw out what isn't. Pitzen says he knew almost immediately that the section about the village was good. "At least that part of the story was kind of inspired by something—I have no idea what."

Whatever that inspiration, it's what makes good writing good. By starting with a specific event that moved him, and remaining open to whatever developed as he wrote, Pitzen got in touch with his muse. He allowed the story to come up from within himself, and the result was an added dimension that lifted the story above the ordinary.

Cecil Grounded

Nothing to it, Cecil said to himself while the stick jolted crazily in his hand and the engine made its final throaty coughs. He cleared the Goebels's barn by eight feet, then dropped, didn't see now how he'd ever make it over the jagged farmhouse shingles and into the meadow beyond; so he fought the stick hard left and tried to hold her to the tractor path running into Goebels's corn. It's all right, he yelled inside his head, the engine dead now and only the wind roaring in his ears, pounding insistently through the flaps of his aviator's cap but refusing to tell him a damn thing. So he thought nothing when the wheels set down on the earth with a knock that sent his jaw nigh through his nose, and only *Lord,* this single word of prayer, as the plane crashed through the corn: stalks snapping around him, dust and severed leaves drifting onto the shuddering wings and into his face. Then the only sounds were the hiss from the engine, voiceless sighs and crackles (death rattle of the broken plants), and the thunder of blood in his own head.

Goebels and his wife were already out of the house, running, when Cecil stepped through the corn. He raised his hands over his head and grinned at them. Grinned because there was nothing else to do; because he was alive; because he'd just pictured the hysteria he must have caused buzzing the farmhouse: rattling the dishes in Mrs. Goebels's breakfront, scaring the farmhouse dogs into corners; and grinning because, after all, there'd been nothing to it.

Goebels was the first to reach him. Cecil thought the farmer had been cussing or mumbling something along the way, but he was only smacking his lips over a lunch left at table. "You hurt?"

"No sir. Not one bit."

"Your lip's bleeding."

Cecil tasted blood and grinned. "Must of bit it some."

"Criminy Moses. What happened up there?"

He shrugged. "Can't say exactly. Could be a busted fuel line."

"This happen before? You ever land on a whim like this before?"

"No sir, this is the first time Maybelline's gotten that idea."

Now Mrs. Goebels was beside her husband, and Cecil could grin and say. "Sorry about the corn, Ma'am. Looks like I owe you a few ears."

"Corn?" Her voice floated up like the toot of a penny whistle. "Don't talk about corn, when all the time running I kept thinking what was I going to tell your parents. Ringing them up to say you'd died in my cornfield."

Cecil said he was sorry for the scare, sorry too that he'd left a ten-acre swath undusted when the problem started. The Goebels walked him to the house, but he wouldn't go inside on account of the dirt and the chemicals coating his clothes and his hair. So they fed him a lunch on the porch. Mrs. Goebels came out to hand him a slice of ice for his lip one minute, a steaming cup of coffee the next. The fuss both embarrassed and tickled him. Overall, it seemed a good thing after the wind's roar in his ears and the stick bucking in his hands like something alive.

From the Goebels's porch he could see Maybelline's tail. Broken corn stalks dangled sorrowfully on either side of the plane's five-yard furrow, some leaves and whitish silks dripped from the stabilizers—making it look like the furry tail of some animal asleep in its burrow.

Finally he and Goebels went to look her over. Now Cecil felt in control again, not angry, ready to forgive Maybelline her pique or illness, ready to start over from scratch. He lifted the cowling and poked around.

"Is she broke?" Goebels asked.

Coming down he must have cracked a couple of struts in the undercarriage; the plane was listing heavily to the left. As for the engine, he could conclude only, "Too hot to see much."

"We'll have to pull her out. Rain's coming in, too."

"Wet don't matter," Cecil said.

Goebels told him that his tractor already had disks mounted behind so he wanted to turn over the twenty acres as he'd planned before pulling them off and hitching the tractor to May-belline. He said he'd park her next to the barn, but if it rained before he got to her, she'd probably be drier in the corn anyway.

"Lor-raine!" Goebels shouted, leaning inside the kitchen door with Cecil standing behind him watching the purple streaks in the eastern sky and stamping both boots to knock off the foul-smelling dust. "What we going to do about Cecil Perkins? Take him on as scarecrow?"

"I guess he's stuck all right," she answered, unseen.

Goebels slammed the screen shut. "Lorraine'll drive you home." He folded his arms over the denim pockets on his chest and stared into his battered corn. "That must of took some flying, bringing her down that way. Shake you up some?"

"No sir," Cecil said. "I had no doubts she'd make it down, just didn't know how slow or fast."

Goebels gave a wheezy laugh. "I hope it ain't broke bad. You do a real good job with that machine. Everybody says so. Course your brother's regarded the famous one in your family, but no-body's got a bad word to say for you neither, Cecil, and that's the truth."

"I guess I know it," he said for something to say.

Once again in motion, with an engine roaring smoothly and a wind that, if he'd cared to lower the glass, could only be whis-tling, Cecil leaned back luxuriously alive in the front seat of the Goebels's big Packard and let the farmer's still-pretty wife ask him questions about Emmett Wayne—which was fine, which was best, which was like sharing something better than you between you, the way some folks could wear your ear about Jesus Christ or President Roosevelt, or the pilots in Little Rock could light up about Ford Tri-Motors.

"What's he studying there?"

RICHARD PLANT

. . . .

141

"Politics. 'Course he takes classes in lots of subjects, math and chemistry and classics and such, but the main one's politics."

"He could be Governor."

"Might could," Cecil agreed out of real feeling and not just politeness. And he went on to describe his younger brother's wins in high school debate, the speech he wrote for commencement; described how Principal West had found himself short-handed one year and hired Wayne to teach a class of eighth graders before Wayne had even graduated high school himself.

But there were some things he didn't tell, details that emerged then settled back into his mind, unspoken, like the dust he saw in the car's side mirror, swirling and settling silently behind them. Cecil sometimes sent Wayne money, and Wayne sent back letters, different from the ones his parents received. These were meant only for him, Cecil, and carried Wayne's own voice on the slanted backs of his spidery ciphers: "I fell asleep to some *Fall and Decline,* woke to what I thought was the stomp of Roman legions, but was only Josh Hoppe drunk upstairs teaching his roommate the tango. If college is the gateway to high culture, it sure seems funny that Yale men are reduced to dancing with other men, more like lonely cowboys or lumberjacks." Or, on another occasion: "Fred McDeal (Ohio man) drove me down to New York last weekend. Wish you could have seen the airfield we passed. More planes than Arkansas has cars! Big passenger birds, too. I have seen the future and it's you, boy." But these were months old.

"Wayne was my alarm clock in summer," Cecil was saying instead. He told Lorraine Goebels about rising before dawn to dig fish bait, how it was Wayne's job to wake him, and so the first thing he'd see at four a.m. would be the kerosene lantern on the floor, hot from burning all night, and Wayne in the opposite bed leaning toward him and hissing his name, a book lying face down on Wayne's lap like a cat he'd stroked to sleep and didn't want to wake.

"Neither of our boys seems much taken with books," Lorraine Goebels said, sighing a mother's sigh.

Before this remark, Cecil had been thinking how much younger than her husband Mrs. Goebels looked, idly sketching out a story of child bride, bored and lonesome. In the fantasy he'd scripted, after a minute's silence Lorraine would begin to sing "Flat Foot Floogie with a Floy Floy," tilting her head forward just enough to smooth out the faint creases under her chin and casting wayward glances at the miraculously spared young flyer beside her. With a thin show of weariness she might propose that they pull over at the Negro jukejoint a mile this side of the Perkins house on the county road for a quick sad song from Lester Lincoln's guitarbox and a cool glass of shine. But of course these things didn't transpire, so when she stopped in front of the desolate barnlike structure Cecil was a little reluctant to call his home, he only thanked her and asked her to tell Goebels to look for him that evening.

"Give your family our best," she said. "And when you write your brother make sure he knows we wish him well."

"Thanks," he said. "I guess I'll see you."

The Packard rolled on toward town while Cecil stood in front of his house, trying to decide what to do first. About the plane, he'd best call Willet Yoates. Yoates was a farmer and self-employed mechanic who had originally bought the Martin biplane from Alvin Barlowe, the bank president, when the bank had started to slip under. Yoates already owned the fastest automobile and the strongest tractor in two counties and couldn't resist owning an aeroplane as well. But Yoates had it only for four years. Then his wife, Clarissa, discovered that the bottom half of their wheat wasn't getting plowed since Willet never had enough gas in the tractor to plow it, and he never had enough gas because he used it for Saturday joyrides in Maybelline. So for $1,750, paid out over three years, Willet Yoates sold his aeroplane to Cecil, who still lived at home then and worked in his father's brick kiln, making extra money from his fishbait business (which he could now recall in detail, perhaps because Maybelline had put his present vocation in jeopardy: getting up at four to dig the nightcrawlers that he sold to fishermen at sunrise, seated on a clover hummock by the side of the dirt turn-off to Carson Lake, his commodity squirming beside him in tin buckets).

Yoates had taught him to fly and take care of Maybelline, which came easy to someone as hand-minded as Cecil. He had given Cecil his leather cap at no charge; he would have thrown in his gloves, but they were too small for Cecil's big hands.

In Little Rock Cecil was certified by a man whose pilot's license had been signed by Orville Wright himself.

"Where you going to keep that thing?" his father had asked. And just the sight of it hulking out back was nearly all it took to make his mother cry with worry. So he'd bought this land on the edge of town and built a hangar for it, and this took so much of his time that he put up a board shack for himself and just started living out here. In spite of all these investments, he'd somehow managed to keep from spending his last cent, and after his father and his brother DeForrest both put in some money he'd wrangled a start in the crop-dusting business, probably because folks had always trusted him to do a good sturdy job, just as they trusted the sun to set in the west and the frogs to sing when it did.

Wayne's letters he kept in a cardboard box on the shelf beside the coffee can he filled with spare coins. And because Lorraine Goebels's well-wishes were more concrete and resonant than his fuzzy projections for fixing Maybelline or otherwise working out the day's remainder, he took these down. The last letter, now a week old, had been the most troubling of the series, tainting Cecil's eager encomiums with a ragged temptation to worry.

"Dear Cecil," it had begun. "I am well and hope you and the folks are the same. Give them my love." But then, instead of the worldly anecdotes and ironic asides he was used to gleaning, nurturing, and then scattering through town like wildflower seeds or insecticide dust, Cecil had read another, serious sort of message:

I'm writing to you because you have always been so strong in my eyes and secretly so much wiser than your snot-nosed brother who went away to Yale and now is cracking up. How do I describe this? I go to class as always, get on with my professors, but more and more I have less and less to say. There is a nervousness in my head that's been building like a boiler fire. Professors Wharton and Summers deduce that I'm ill prepared, that I don't read the texts, that I lack the necessary interest. Now I confide in you what I couldn't explain to them. You, Cecil, know I need no great excuse to exercise my eyes by lamplight. The pages are still turning, but my brain is losing its grip. I no longer have ideas. I can't even remember where ideas come from. And when I am presented with two ready-made ideas and asked to make a choice, I cannot. I don't remember how to judge.

On occasion I've flat looked ridiculous in class, mumbling apologies or proffering ludicrous guesses when called upon. But my fears are even worse: every day I sit at the end of a row of scholars and drive my spine down into the hard wood of my seat while I wait in terror for the sound of my name. If a professor calls me out I shall certainly scream, or gurgle unintelligible baby sounds while the rest of the class looks on, horrified.

When other students speak I am amazed. Where do they find the words and how do they know the proper sequence? I feel like applauding. I feel like all these other men find words magically etched across the glowing curve of their skull, while my eyes look in and see only darkness, an empty black cavern where the wind whistles through empty crannies and corners and bounces back from nothing at all.

Cecil, I can't imagine how this looks to you. I read it once and see that I have exaggerated my problem unforgivably. I read it a second time and find this account only a pale reflection of my terror. I don't mean to frighten you. I think I'm telling you this so that now I can afford myself the comforting picture of you holding my letter in your big hands, giving your head a pragmatic shake of disgust and telling me to remember who I am and what I am. Tell me this latest crisis is just a twinge of being sensitive to the point of womanly weakness. And even though you're there in Arkansas, I want to feel you shake me and slug me with your brick-baking, cloud-hopping hands, knocking the fluff out of my skull and putting me to rights.

Already I feel some relief. I trust you not to speak of this to Mom or Dad. My next letter, I hope, will be none of this sop but some real news.

Love, Wayne

After he had read this letter through the first time, a week ago, Cecil had opened the door of his handmade house and watched the sun slip off the edge of the blood-tinted cotton field across the road. Tomorrow should be good weather for dusting, he had figured. Little or no wind—the dust would be allowed to nestle into Sharp's corn like snow; then if his almanac was right, there would be rain later in the week to tamp it down.

Cecil had gone back in the house and read the letter a second time. Finally he put it down, stroked his long, stubbly jaw, and grinned. Hadn't he always known his brother Emmett Wayne to be the family genius, and didn't this high-pitched letter just confirm it all again? Cecil had never been to college himself, but vaguely knew that great men at college were supposed to experience crises of the heart and soul, lose God and then find him in another shape, and finally emerge viewing the world in a light and a language above the murky understanding of the common man—the common man being himself, Cecil. What else, he had tried to persuade himself, did Wayne expect of him but a slap and a grin?

Cecil found some hosing, clamps, and copper tubing easily enough in the nest of materials that had accumulated against the north wall of his aeroplane hangar. So before dark he'd wrestled a new fuel line into Maybelline's innards and gotten her to burn, without dying, a full gallon of petrol. But the rejuvenated engine rocked violently and uncharacteristically to one side, and Cecil had no idea why. Also, in dragging the plane from the corn to the lee of his barn, Goebels had done further damage to the broken landing gear, a mangled mess of splintered wood and twisted brackets that could only be replaced, not repaired.

Over the telephone in the Goebels's kitchen, where bare-armed Lorraine was kneading dough for her Saturday dumplings, Cecil, a stranger in this house, heard the disembodied voice of Clarissa Yoates; so that for an instant he could fancy himself capable of transcending the normal laws of space and time and maybe even sex, flitting from the tinkling voice of one woman to the sight (and smell?) of another.

"Willet's gone to Shreveport, Cecil. His brother there passed on last night."

"I'm real sorry," he said, suddenly small and mortal again.

She explained that the funeral was to be in two days, but Willet was likely to stay longer. "What was it you wanted?"

"It's no real matter," he said. "I thought maybe Willet would like to dirty his hands on Maybelline once more, but it'll wait. Is there something I can do for you folks?"

She said no, but would call him if there was. Cecil did not explain that his own house did not have a phone. He hung up, smiled his thanks to Mrs. Goebels, and before spreading the Yoates tragedy before her, shrugged at his own relatively comic share of misfortune and declared, "I'm grounded."

"You must think I'm tracking you." This was Cecil's greeting when he stepped through the barber's door and saw Goebels there with his youngest.

"Hi-you, Cecil. Lance here's getting too shaggy for Mama's taste. You know Mr. Perkins, son?"

"You fly the aeroplane."

"Yessir. Gus, you going to give ole Lance a shave today?" All three of the waiting chairs were filled, so Cecil sprawled in the black, wrought-iron shoeshine seat. Not yet noon and already the Saturday bucks had started to slink in for their haircuts and shaves, for a sprinkle of witch hazel on the back of the neck and behind the ears. Cecil was amused, although he was himself a courting sort of buck, though come to it late.

"I hear you taught that aeroplane some tricks, Cecil," Gus teased.

"She's a puppy dog. I say 'git' and she goes. I say 'roll over' and she do."

"What'd you say in Val Goebels's cornfield?"

"Play dead."

As the men chortled he pictured Maybelline listing against the side of Goebels's barn, shrouded in a canvas tarpaulin, and Willet Yoates bowed at graveside somewhere in Louisiana.

One buck, a teenager named Mitch'L Leeds, picked up the banter. "Perkins, you pay Gus extra to scrape all them poor squashed flies, gnats, and nits off your face?"

Cecil had a reputation as a man who loved a good ribbing, to give or receive. "Mitch'L," he said, "you so soft, you go up in an aeroplane for five minutes with those little buggies slapping your face, I bet you come down looking like a bruised banana. I bet they knock you senseless."

"You was born senseless," Mitch'L replied.

"That's likely true."

"They held back his brains so Emmet Wayne could have a double dose," Gus said.

"I think that's so, and one smart feller per family suits me fine."

"How's Wayne doing?"

"Stupendous. Him at that college is like Jesus teaching the elders."

"He's a genius," Mitch'L Leeds said flatly, as though he were giving the time of day. "I went through school with him."

Shorn and bored, Lance turned to his father in the chair beside his. "What's *genius?*"

"Smarts, boy."

"Brains."

"Kentucky quarterhorse running in his traces."

"Might could be President."

"It means," Cecil said, looking serious, "when my little brother rides through this here town on his presidential train with the banners waving and the bands a-playing, the squirrels in the trees and the pigs in their sty better nod politely to him or else."

"Else what?"

"Else I'll pick them right up and make them nod," he shouted, bounding from the shoeshine dais, the iron chair vibrating as though struck by a violent wind—"Like this"—plucking the boy from the barber chair into the cradle of his arms, swinging the open-mouthed towhead back and forth, the barber's towel twisted and flapping.

"You!" shrieked the boy. "Hey you!"

Outside, Cecil could feel stray hairs creeping down his overalls, his shirt collar, teasing his skin like little shivers of ice. If he had any brains, he'd invent a new kind of barber's bib to protect customers from this lingering itch. As he paused, bending to brush the loose hairs from his head and face, Cecil heard a snuffle and moan. He took a peek down the alley behind the barber shop's west wall and saw a familiar dark huddle on the ground, shivering in the shadow of the bricks.

"Hey you, Lester."

The huddle raised its head but continued to shake. "What that?"

Cecil leaned into the alley. With one arm he pulled Lester Lincoln to his feet. "All right?"

The thin black man's head wobbled from side to side. He refused to raise his focus from the ground, as though that seat had become a warm, fondly remembered place. "Ain't me," he rasped, the words punched from inside.

Cecil pulled him gently into the sunlight and, satisfied that this dark skeleton could stand, released his arm and pressed some money into his palm. "Look here, Lester. Shaking so bad you could jar the bricks from this wall, be like Joshua's trumpet at Jericho. Now take this four-bits and buy yourself a drink."

Lester stared at the coins and finally tilted an eye up at Cecil. It almost made Cecil shiver himself, this glassy yellow puddle threaded with red, cocked up at him from a body that trembled like a thing possessed. "You a Christian man."

"May be," Cecil said. "But I suspect the dog what bit you done also snapped at me."

Cecil took the boardwalk in long, driving strides, testing the stretch and balance of his own muscles now, proving himself king of his own big body: sharp and strong, chewing the planks beneath his heels, spitting them out behind him.

The Eubanks Grocery reminded Cecil of a well-stocked cave, cool and clean and fragrant. When he heard the shiny pine floorboards creak and shift beneath his weight, he thought instead of ships at sea and tilting decks. He bought a pound of sugar-cured bacon, apples, bread, canned beans, and wine. He teased the butcher for his cleaver's dullness, juggled apples for the register girl, and—full of himself once more—took up Eubanks's challenge to move the pickle barrel four feet to the south. There was a mousehole behind it they needed to stuff. The men waited until the store's other two customers left, then Eubanks closed the door and put Cecil's purchases next to the register.

"Don't hurt yourself."

"No chance," he said. "I waltz with barrels bigger than this in my sleep." The pickle barrel had water up to a foot from the top. He first tried to lift it by reaching around the highest metal hoop, which felt wonderfully cool but was too slick to grasp. So he squatted once more and this time hugged the staves beneath, pushing in until his wrists, his forearms, and his shoulders all tingled from the pressure. Nothing to it, he said behind clenched teeth. Then, straightening his legs, he hoisted it off the floor and tottered the necessary three steps while the floorboards sang in complaint. Some of the pickle water sloshed out when he set the barrel down, making a dark place on the shiny wood. They cheered him—Fred the butcher, Eubanks, and the girl who ran the register—and Eubanks reopened the street door.

"Don't ring up those apples, Grace. This lunkhead earned those at least."

Cecil rubbed his wrists and winked at the girl.

"You're Wayne Perkins's brother."

"I guess I must be."

"Hear from him much?"

"Now and then. Want me to say hi?"

"From Grace," she said, smiling. "I played clarinet in high school band."

"I don't recollect Wayne playing in band."

"Well, no, but that's probably the only way he'd remember me. I never stood out much but for the clarinet."

Cecil smiled back at this girl with the single talent and promised to mention her in the next letter.

Clouds were moving in. Cecil stood on the boardwalk with his bag of groceries, his clipped hair prickling the back of his neck, and watched the clouds. He sniffed for rain. It had missed them last night but wouldn't be long in coming now. Cecil was excited by the prospect of rain, the challenge of dodging showers long enough to pick up Patrice and make his parents' house without getting soaked.

Somehow informed of his trouble at Goebels's, Cecil's mother would likely start up on the dangers of flying, citing once more—this time for Patrice's benefit—the deaths of Wiley Post and Will Rogers, Amelia Earhart slipping into the ocean like a slender, fallen feather. She thought they should ban Jimmie Allen from the radio, prohibit his weekly adventures and tin aeroplane toys from stirring kids up about flying. As though an aeroplane were something wicked. Tonight Cecil would drop his heavy elbows on the table and argue. It's nothing but a machine, Ma. Why do you talk this way? Look, an aeroplane is just metal and wood, wire and petrol. You don't have to talk to it or pray to it or be real smart about it, you just have to know what little lever does what job. An aeroplane is no more mysterious than your own hands and feet, no more mysterious. (And all this time Maybelline would be crouching under a tarpaulin in a strange farmyard, the raindrops coursing across her canvas cover like tears across a face.) To avoid an argument, they'd talk instead about DeForrest, who was in the service, or Wayne, who would soon be home from Yale. He would lose at Hearts after dinner in the room where his stuffed pheasant and Wayne's debating trophy and a picture of DeForrest in uniform crowded the mantel. He and Patrice would excuse themselves to go to the picture show, but instead they would huddle together in his buggy, away from the rip in the roof, and head for Cecil's house on the outskirts of town. There they would shuck their wet clothes by candlelight and go to bed with the drops hitting the roof tiles and spattering against the windows and, likely as not, leaking through to pop on the floorboards like sparks from a fire. Racing the rain tonight would be like racing against gravity before lifting off in Maybelline.

Patrice was busy behind the post office counter weighing packages for an old-timer with a cane, so Cecil stood with his hands behind his back reading the familiar Wanted posters. Dillinger had been gone for years. Now there was round-headed Franklin Dobbs, sought for kidnapping. Armed and dangerous. What crime would he, Cecil, be most likely to join this roster of the infamous for? The F.B.I. did not waste their time and bullets on mere fornicators, show-offs, men who flew too close to the ground.

He turned and opened the door for the old man.

"You got a letter," Patrice said and disappeared behind the wall of silver-trimmed mailboxes. Cecil leaned on the counter; tried to pick out the smell of her.

"Here," she said, returning. "I was going to bring it tonight."

"Isn't that a crime, taking other folks' mail?"

Patrice leaned over her side of the counter. With her face beside his, she whispered, "You could lead me into a life of crime, Cecil DeLoss Perkins. Deep into it."

Cecil felt the top of his ear getting hot, there where Gus had clipped the hair close to his head. "It's fixing to rain. I should be by early."

She said, "Yes. You better."

He could hear someone step up behind him, so he straightened and asked for three stamps.

"Here. Nine cents."

"You say *nonsense?*" He spoke loudly, in feigned confusion. She wrinkled her forehead and pursed her lips in a crooked pucker. He found the coins in his bib pocket and pressed the last penny into Patrice's hand slowly, all four fingers curled into her open palm, caressing her fingertips as he lifted, turned, and left.

Cecil read Wayne's new letter seated in his buggy.

New Haven
April 29, 1938

Dear Cecil,

Things are getting worse. I may have to get help. The last two days I went to class but got nothing from the lectures. I know the teachers are speaking, I can see their lips move. But I can't make sense of the sounds that come out. I'm supposed to study for final exams. I'm looking over these notes that read now like something written by another person.

I think different people peak at different times. Mozart peaked early and Beethoven later in life. I've peaked and am now sinking fast. Maybe high school was my peak. At the regional debate tournament I delivered my rebuttal without even looking at my notes or pausing to think of a next sentence. They just came to me, gifts. I was like a spigot running full blast. And while I was speaking I did not lose a beat but felt like I moved outside myself and watched myself and it was wonderful. This sounds vain or stupid, I know, but it was a moment when I felt in love with myself and grateful I could filter ideas out of thin air. And now all I feel is a dread, a sinking into silence and ignorance. The spigot is shut off. I hope to limp through finals and come home. I want to come home very much. But I must pull myself together first. Mother and Dad can't see me like this. It's a frightened dead stone that I've become. Pray.

Love, Wayne

The air's moisture made Cecil's cotton shirt feel clammy before the first drops even fell. He tried to concentrate on the grayness of the horizon, on the rhythm of the hoofbeats, on the intervals between lightning flashes in the clouds—not on his brother's letter nor on the reply that before returning to town for Patrice he'd carefully scrawled and stamped:

Dear Wayne,

Ignorance is no sin in my book. I hope you feel better about yourself. You have worked too hard and need a rest. Come home now. Grace who plays clarinet says hello. Here is fifteen dollars.

Love, Cecil

But since these diversions did not work, he tried to concentrate on Patrice, who leaned into his side but was quiet.

Although *loneliness* was a word Cecil had little truck with, sometime after Wayne had gone to school and he had moved out to his home-hangar, loneliness had begun to eat big holes in him, holes that flying and liquor and ribbing couldn't fill. He needed a woman was all. So when Patrice Jackson showed him that first sign of tenderness he had jumped for her like a startled buck jumps for the safety of trees. And she was sweet to him, lord she was sweet. She knew what he liked without even saying: such as pulling off her long stockings, like peeling a clean, sweet piece of fruit. When he had little to say she let him sit silent with no bother nor worried little bird-glances. And he never told her so, but he liked the way in bed her hands would push against his chest, not pushing him away but lying open against him and following him like flowers follow the power of the wind.

On Tuesday, Willet Yoates was still in Louisiana and it was still raining. Cecil should have been dusting five hundred acres ten miles east of the river. The cotton field across the way was saturated, water spilling from its furrows onto the road like parallel creeks emptying into a single river. He could look between the porch planks, through cracks under his feet, and see floating twigs, the dull reflection of water.

It was a quiet rain. Loudest was the drumming it made on the big chemical mixing tank behind the house. Cecil heard the bicycle's squeak before he looked down the road and saw the boy and the bicycle. The Western Union boy's yellow slicker was the only thing of color, the boy and the bicycle the only things moving under the dark blanket of rain. When the boy came alongside Cecil's house, he looked up. Now he knows I've been standing here watching him, Cecil thought. The boy looked more angry than miserable as he stomped to Cecil's porch, rain running off his hat brim and mud oozing from under his boots.

"Telegram," he said, opening a hard leather case on his belt and handing Cecil the paper. He said the words like a challenge, like something nobody should have to ride two miles in the rain to pronounce to a big man in his bare feet with nothing better to do than stand on his rickety porch and watch boys getting soaked, but he had done all that anyway, so there.

"Come in," Cecil said. The boy took off his hat and hit it against the porch rail. He had red hair, matted high on his forehead. The boy followed Cecil far enough for Cecil to shut the door behind him, then shivered once, like a wet dog. "I have some coffee," Cecil said, but went instead to his money can and picked out a dime for the boy.

"Yessir. Why don't you read it," the boy said. "You might want to send an answer."

CECIL STOP CHECKED INTO HOSPITAL FOR MENTAL STOP WILL NOT BE HOME NEXT WEEK AS PLANNED STOP SCHOOL WANTS TO INFORM PARENTS BUT I AM TELLING YOU INSTEAD STOP MAKE SOMETHING UP FOR ME STOP DONT WORRY STOP WAYNE

When he looked up, Cecil was surprised to see the Western Union boy still there, looking at him. "There's no answer," he said. The boy opened the door himself and went back out into the rain.

Cecil took a wet rag and cleaned the floor where the boy had stood in his muddy boots, then worked on the rest of the house, pushing the rag in long, furious strokes. When he finally straightened up to shove his bed aside, there was a cramp hammering at his back. He took down the whiskey bottle and kept it open beside him. He carried his three rugs outside and shook them out, flapping them one at a time up and down like a giant bat wing; little swirls of dust became airborne in the gray rain.

Inside the house he washed his drinking glasses. He emptied the whiskey bottle into a clean glass, and after he'd drunk that down washed the glass a second time.

Soon after, he heard the porchboards creak, the door swing open, and there was Patrice. She tracked red mud in his doorway, but her hat and her shoulders looked dry. The rain had let up.

"I wish you'd get a damn telephone out here."

"Hello," he said.

"You got a telegram from Connecticut. Is everything all right?"

Cecil felt like shouting at her, demanding to know how it was that every weakness in his life became public knowledge, how news traveled so fast through thin air and became bad news only from the grime of ears and tongues it touched on its way. Then he remembered that Patrice worked in the post office, and that the Western Union desk was also in the post office. He said, "Is that why you're here?"

"I was a little worried, yes." She had taken off her hat and coat and hung them by the door. Now she was unlacing her shoes.

"Wayne," Cecil said, as he felt the story making itself up and cutting sharply through the whiskeyweight on his tongue, "was asked to help a teacher with some research project. It's an honor and it pays. So he's not coming home next week like we thought."

"Is that all?" Patrice pushed her hair back with her fingers and smiled at him.

"Yeah," he said. "Excuse me a minute." He made a sweep with his hand, something to indicate *Would you sit down? Help yourself? Whatever the hell you want.* Then he went out the back door. The stones that led to the outhouse were cold under his bare feet. They were also slick with mud, and Cecil was a little unsteady from the whiskey. He nearly fell.

The rain smelled like something alive.

Cecil closed the door. He sat to the right of the shithole, rounded and black beside him like a grin, and pressed his shoulder against the outhouse wall. Now I must make this something I can touch, something I can carry, he argued. After all, he was made to carry loads. His back was strong, his hands were strong, he was made of muscle and bone and will. Cecil pulled on his lower lip with his teeth, trying to taste the whiskey again. He could board a train for the East tonight, run down a moving box-car outside of Shantytown if need be, and get there by Thursday. He could find Emmett Wayne and haul him right out of that hospital, lift him up with these hands, heft him over his shoulder. He could plow through whitecoats as if playing high school football. He could carry Wayne home like a conqueror.

What a strong and wonderful picture of himself, clearer now than the black earth between his feet. Isn't this what Wayne would expect of him, and so what he had to do? This vision hovered just overhead, tugging him after. And the warm whiskey was expanding and pushing him out of himself, up toward the vision. Then between these two forces, not trying too hard, he felt his spirit pushing out at his taut shoulders, pushing out at his neck, jumping with a frenzy he never expected of his own lazy, half-lidded soul. Now he could feel it ooze free, rising two or three wobbly feet in the outhouse dark. Cecil DeLoss looked down. What he saw was his own big agonized self all bent and heaving with a wet glisten on the hair of his forearms. He heard himself moan, and his soul slipped back in like a kiss.

Notes

Two things make "Cecil Grounded" work: the first is the voice. Cecil is both down-to-earth and poetic, a born storyteller. He makes you want to hear what he has to say.

That, in fact, is how this story came to be. Cecil and Wayne first appeared as minor characters in an earlier Richard Plant story. "After the first story, I felt I wasn't through with those folks yet," he says. "In particular I wanted to hear more of Cecil's voice."

So he began writing a second story, and found Cecil speaking up. "This story would come to me in sentences and I had this voice I was working out of," he says. "I don't really know how, but through whatever means, I hit a voice that is compelling and credible."

The other aspect that's important to "Cecil Grounded" is the setting. "I felt like I was describing a real place and creating this world that I felt comfortable in, and I could imagine my characters moving and speaking and acting in that world," Plant says. "So it was the characters and the setting too that for some reason had this pull on me and helped me write the story. I was just there."

Robert Fogarty, editor of the *Antioch Review,* says the setting was for him the most striking factor, particularly in the opening scene. "The juxtaposition of this marvelous thing happening in a landscape that is familiar. . . . That was probably the most unusual thing about that story."

The vivid landscape and the sure voice combined to make the story come alive, Fogarty says. "You're struck immediately by the fact that the story is well crafted and has a certain impact. One gets off the page—one is no longer reading the story, but is indeed involved and experiencing what the writer wants you to experience."

Plant says the setting and characters had an "uncommon appeal" for him. "Partly, I think, because the Arkansas crop duster and his Ivy League brother, life in the rural thirties, were all so removed from my own time, place, and experiences that they seemed to invite—and sustain—my myth-making."

The characters aren't based on real people, Plant says, "except for being based on little parts of me. I feel like I'm kind of fragmented in that story. There's a piece of me in this character, and there's a piece of me in that character, but not all of me in any of the characters."

Plant says the story not only invited his myth-making, but is in part *about* myth-making. The townspeople in the story help create Wayne's image, and seem to need him to succeed. "I can imagine a whole town getting energy from a representative who's out there in the world achieving what, in their eyes, would be great things."

But even though the story helped propel Plant, writing it wasn't simple. He began it while in the writing program at Washington University, and it underwent a couple of major revisions and several minor ones before being published.

The most important of those changes involved the opening scene. Originally the story began with the scene in the barber shop and the plane crash took place off stage. Other students in his fiction workshop told Plant the opening was limp. "It was like the Andy Griffith show—the good old boys sitting around jawing in the barber shop. You didn't know what the focus of the story was going to be and there wasn't enough tension," Plant says.

So he decided to use the plane crash. But since he'd never flown in a 1930s crop-dusting plane, Plant tried to research the topic. He didn't find much other than names of aircraft from that period, so the scene "is mostly guesswork," he says.

"That's one thing that excites me about writing, to try to describe an experience you've never had and probably won't ever have—to try on that other life for a while."

After the revisions, "Cecil Grounded" was rejected three times before the *Antioch Review* accepted it. Fogarty says the decision was easy. "We read it, we liked it, and we took it."

Plant was not so nonchalant. "The acceptance letter came on a rainy day in May. I remember the day because that same afternoon, a farmer in a rusted pickup rammed my car in an intersection and we had to stand by our vehicles in the rain, waiting for the police. Despite the rain and the minor accident, I was probably smiling: I was going to be published!"

It was a moment Plant had been working toward for a long time. He says he has been writing "forever." "I can remember typing stories on my mother's typewriter before I knew how to type. I remember sitting on a telephone book and hitting the keys to write short stories."

He has also written poetry and essays. After "Cecil Grounded" was published, he was contacted by several agents and the story was selected for *Prize Stories 1988: The O. Henry Awards.*

"That was terribly exciting and of course a great motivator to produce more and keep working at it," Plant says.

And he has. But he's not sure he's through with Cecil yet. "I still don't feel free of these characters, these lives, although I've certainly written other kinds of stories since," he says. "A part of me's itching to get Cecil airborne again."

Babies

It was good fuckin shit, not that second rate stuff; it was really good shit, the kind you pay a lot for, so I stared at Smiley for a while cause I got real curious bout where the money came from.

"What," he said, lookin at me while he rolled another joint.

"Where you get the money, macho?" I axed him, an he started backin up into the riot gate we were standin in front of.

"Aw c'mon, don't start."

"Me start?" I yelled real loud, cause I knew it bugged him whenever I did that on the street an everyone knew our problems. "I'm not startin nothin, I juss wanna know where you got the money, whachu been husslin."

"It wasn't no hussle, muñeca, juss chill out."

"Yeah, yeah, I heard that before, man. If the fuckin cops come snoopin aroun the house for your ass again Smiley man, thass it, we're through. I don't wanna fuckin hassle with that no more."

"Shut up an like, smoke."

I'm serious, Smiley got some real special shit, don't taste like tree bark. We smoked an hung out for a while, then Smiley went to the Super to see bout maybe gettin some work cause usually Smiley could get somethin to do like plumbin or puttin up a cielin someplace an then we could have money for rent. The goddamn foodstamps ran out. Now we're in some real serious shit. I din't know before but when I went upstairs with my friend Sara I saw the empty book. I'll tell you somethin else we ain't got: food. I checked in the fridge an the bastid's empty, even the light bulb quit on us. It smells all funny in there, all mildewy, an there's some green shit growin in the egg tray an clusters of dead roaches floatin in the dingy water at the bottom. There's a half-empty box of Sugar Pops. Dinner.

Check it out, Smiley don't really care bout food anyway. When we first moved in together he knew I coodent cook for shit but he said fuck it cause he wanted his favrit piece of ass with him. (Thass my sentimental Smiley!) There's no house cleanin either cause there ain't much of a house, juss a two-room apartment on the fifth floor that came complete with a matress. (We still use it but we washed it first.) We got a small black an white tv set, a love seat that smells funny an has a paint can for a fourth leg, an an old bureau we grabbed off the street that came complete with its very own roaches. (Free! Where else but in America?) Thass all our furniture. We got a grey exercise mat we use like a dinin area on the floor so when people come to eat they gotta sit on the floor like chinks or those hindoos.

Sara hung out with me for a while until we finished the last joint. She has a radio; it's really her man's but she carries it aroun anyway. She played it while we sat by the window cause it was spring an the breeze was cool an fresh. Sara is kinda dark, but she's Rican, with good hair, not grifo, it's long an soft. She's gotten a little fat, but then she had a baby bout two weeks ago an she's still drippin.

"Where's the baby anyway?" I axed, thinkin bout that little dark bundle I saw wrapped tightly in blue at Lincoln Hospital, when she had it an I went to visit.

"It's aroun," she said tiredly, not wantin to talk bout it.

"Where aroun?"

"I think Madgie's with him outside the bakery. Or maybe I leff him by the liquor store. I dunno." She shrugged like there was a bug on her shoulder.

"Man, you gotta cut that shit out," I said without too much conviction. "You're a mother now," I added, feelin it was the right thing to say an shit. "You gotta be responsible an take care of your baby."

"I know," she said loud, forehead all pruned up. "I know that! What, you think I don't know that?" you think I treat my baby mean? He hangs out with me all the time! All the time, dammit, he's there, remindin me!" She lay back on our dinin mat. "Shit. Tell me I don't take care a my kid. I bet if you had a kid, you do better?"

I din't say nothin cause I knew she was all crotchity bout that kid. This always happens with her, so like always, I juss let her blow all her steam out. You could tell it was botherin her. Her man (not the one with the radio, he's the NEW man), I mean the father of the kid, at first seemed hip to the idea of the boy but then he got real pissed off. One night, they were outside the liquor store an it was about midnight. They were both drinkin, an they got in a fight. . . . He wanted to know what right she had to fuck up his life. All he knows how to do is drink an stan aroun, he ain't got time for no babies, so what she come with this shit now for? She threw a half-empty bottle of Smirnoff at him, which really upset some of the other winos cause it was such a waste of good drinkin stuff. She got all teary an stood out in the middle of the street with the baby carriage.

"Fuck you!" she screamed, all hoarse. "I don't give a fuck!" An swoosh, a car passed bout three inches from the baby carriage.

"I hope you get kill, bitch!" he screamed back.

A big bus popped up, one of those new air conditioned ones from Japan that look like bullets. It started honking. She swung the baby carriage at it. Thass when I stepped in cause I was out waitin for Smiley an saw the whole thing. I dragged her home an fix her a drink. (Her apartment, by the way, is worse than ours. At least ours has a cielin over the bathroom.) The baby was crying like somebody stepped on it.

"Put this on his face an he'll shut up," she said, handin me a blanket. "It always works."

I took him into the bathroom, the only other room in that dump thass private, an I shut the door on him so his cryin sounded far off an echoey.

"I'm so fucked up!" she wailed. "I lost my man, an here I am stuck with that . . . that . . . ohhh, fuck that bastid! Mother fucker, iss all his fault! To hell with him! Who needs him? You think I need him to bring up the baby? I'll bring it up all on my own, who needs him? That prick. He better gimmie money, ain't no way he's gonna walk out on me an not gimmie money, I don't care if we ain't married, he still has to gimmie money, that bastid. . . ."

"If you don't stop screamin, the baby ain't never gonna shut up an sleep," I said. Her eyes got all wild.

"Din't I tell you," she screamed, "to put a blanket over it? Put a blanket on the baby's head an it'll shut up!"

Everything was quiet for a while as we sat under the window an her mouth got sick of screamin. When the joint finished, she turned on the radio to WKTU.

"So whachu name the baby?" I axed, now that the storm was over. She was lyin on our dinin mat like a corpse, her eyes cuttin holes in the cielin. "Baby," she said. "It's called Baby."

I grimaced. "Thass stupid."

"Fuck you, juss whachu know about babies?"

Okay: I know that I got leff in a carriage in the hot sun when I was a baby, my older brother told me. He said my mother got drunk an forgot where I was an hadda go to the hospital. I remember when I was three an my mother was with this man. She got drunk an put a hankie over my eyes so I coodent see, then the two of them spun me aroun an aroun. They sped off in his Camaro, strandin me on Randall's Island for a long time. I got lost an walked aroun an cried a river an cops saw me an took my hands an told me stories until they came back in the Camaro an felt all embarassed. A big Irish cop with a thick moustache got real mad at her, noticed they were both stoned an gave them both tickets. When we got home, my mother beat the livin shit out of me. "It was juss a game," she howled, lookin spurned, "you din't have to go an fuck it up."

"I don't know," I said to Sara. "I'm just fucked up." I got up, away from her. I din't wanna talk bout babies no more. I went to my favrit drawer in the bureau an got my stuff. Sara watched. She liked to watch me shoot up, though she never did H cause she said she didn't wanna die. She juss liked to watch an axe stupid questions like if it was school an I was a tutor. I took out my kit but let it lie for a while cause I was still buzzin from the joint.

I hate it when people say I'm a junkie an shit cause it's really not true. I know I got it under control, an plus I know I can stop anytime I want. (I did once, for three whole days, an then since I knew I could take it or leave it I took it, cause I mean, what else is there? Why shoodent I feel sweet?) Some hispanics even been axin me where I picked up such a habit, cause aroun 149th there ain't no sixteen year old girls on H. The fack is I used to hang out in the village with this funky guy named Matt, who used to do crazy shit like steal cars for a day juss to ride aroun an then dump em somewhere. I met him through a friend in junior high. We used to hang out a lot in that park with the big white arch thing, where he used to deal H to all the junkies who hung out there. An I axed him what it was like to take H cause I seen him sniffin it, an he gimmie a book to read: Christiane F. I read like four pages an said, enough of this shit, I hate books. He got mad an said I should learn somethin, but I woodent go near it again, so he said fuck it, I should learn the hard way then. He shot me full of sweet H. At first I felt like I was gonna throw up on him, my stomach was dribblin aroun an my head felt like if it was seperatin from my body. I got real nervous until Matt told me to relax an not be uptight an then I started feelin real good. The necks day he shot me up again an made a joke bout that bein my last free sample, an when that freeze hit me I was on cloud nine, ten, eleven. I was free of everythin that bugged my head out, like my mother, who was out fuckin like a dog in heat, or my bad grades in school or my older brother, who one day disappeared without even a fuckin poof, leavin a pair of beat up Pro Keds on the kitchen table as a goodbye. Nah, I wasn't thinkin bout nothin at all, juss gettin more sweet H, an takin more trips into that sweet nothin land that took me away from it all. I hadda keep shootin after that. One time I bought some real bad shit from some guy I din't know, a fuckin Boricua dude, an it was awful. I felt like if bugs were crawlin all over an I coodent stop scratchin. That was the only time I ever got fucked up. That was a year ago, that I turned on I mean, an since then I haven't got the sunken face or the bags under the eyes or circles neither; I look great. In fack, guys keep axin me out all the time, but I got Smiley, so I say nah. I'd only be like my mother if I said YEAH.

Smiley's two years older than me. He's tall an sleek, with a
sorta beard that feels nice. He smokes pot like a stove. He
dropped out of high school to work in a car shop on Bruckner
Boulevard. He lived in whass now our place with two other dudes
cause his father hated him an his mother din't really care bout
nothin much. His father would beat her aroun like a ping-pong.
Smiley got sick of it, so one day durin one of his father's drunkin
freakouts, Smiley got a kitchen knife an stabbed him. Yeah, Smiley
stuck him an they threw him in Riker's Island for six months. I
think thass one of the most heroic things I ever heard of in my
life, which is why I really love him, cause he's so sweet an coura-
geous. He met me one day cause of one of his roomies, a thin kid
with a bushy head an a face used to stompins, who used to sit in
my home-room class. Smiley came to hang out with him an he
met me an we started seein each other an got it on, an six months
ago he kicked out his roomies for bein slobs an he axed me to
move in. You bet your ass I did. I leff my alkie-mother on Cypress
Avenue with her roomful of men doin rotatin shifts, her smell all
over the street. For a little while there were fluffy clouds an flowers an romance. I shood end that with one of those happy-ever-
after things like in all great lit, but there's always trouble. Last
summer the cops busted him twice cause he lost his job an did
some husslin; once they caught him with stolen goods, the other
time he got fingered in a muggin. I tried to get him to stop, but
then he has to get his smoke, an I need my H, I get real cranky
without it.

My buzz was fadin out, so I shot up. I lit my juice an shot up
quick, cause Sara was gettin loud, she always does when she gets
high an she juss says the stupidest shit. I juss floated away an only
came back when she mentioned Diana.

Check it out, Diana is this sixteen year old girl who's really
preggoes, like out to here, I don't know how many fuckin months
gone by, she's younger lookin than I am an has a real pretty com-
plexion like a Ivory girl, skin dark an smooth, eyes bright, tiny red
lips that pout, nice narrow waist. The first time I seen her when
she moved in with her mother an little sister I said, this one won't

last. She din't. She got fucked fast enough by this guy everybody knows named Freddie, who thinks he's a fuckin beat boy an acts all bad. Now she's real big, an he's nowhere in sight.

"I know her mother," Sara was saying, walkin aroun real fast. "I talk to her alla time, you know, she like, talks to me, knows I'm a mother too, she's a real slick lady, no shit. Works in Lerner's, that store? The one on Third Avenue man, no shit, she sells dresses." She laughed hysterically for some fuckin reason. I told you, she gets this way when she's on smoke.

"An like she's real decent, up-standin woman, she don't be hangin out with all these scums an shit heads, she got it all together. She really care bout her two girls, which is why issa shame bout Diana. An Marissa be fourteen necks month, now I hope it don't happen to her!"

Yeah, Marissa, fourteen, wears black boots an skin tight pants an waist cords an glossy lipstick an two huge plastic earrings. She's necks. Nah, I don't think it's good for a growin girl to have a mother who works at Lerner's.

"Though I seen her yesterday, she was wearin a mini-skirt with those . . . those wild panty hoses an shit, with the designs? Shit man. Her mother dresses her real good. She's really a mother, you know." She leaned real close to me. "She's tryin to get Diana to get a abortion."

"It's too late," I said, knowin Diana was too far gone for one.

"Yeah, but she knows somebody who'll do it cheap. I tol you girl, I talk to her, she confide in me an shit! I tol her it was the right thing to do. Babies can be death, man. I tol her I shoulda abortioned mines. You know? I axed her if she wanted my baby, but she said nah."

I started laughin. That was really wild!

"I'm serious, muñeca, I really meant it, cause I know she's a good mother."

"An she said no?"

"Yeah."

"You really give your baby away to somebody if they take him?"

"Sure, why not?" she said, gettin up, as if I insulted her or somethin. "She can bring it up good. Give it a good home an toys an money an shit." She wasn't facin me. "I don't wanna talk bout this no more."

"Okay," I said, feelin like I did somethin wrong. "You want some Sugar Pops?" I brought em over from the fridge an dug deep into the box, poppin em into my mouth by hand.

"Nah, I gotta go," she said, an poof, a kiss on the cheek, an she was out the door, with the fuckin radio too.

Talkin to Sara bout babies made me feel funny inside. It's like, I don't know, I think I could be a great mother but sometimes I get into moods where I think I'm too fucked up to even take care of myself, an I don't know enough bout things, an life, an maybe I'll juss fuck up the kid. Those other times when I think I could really swing it an be a good mother are kind of painful, cause it gets like an itch an it makes me wanna swell up right away. I guess cause I was thinkin bout it so much, an cause I was high on H, when Smiley came in late at night I axed him bout babies.

"What about em?" he axed back, rollin a joint as he sat on our dinin mat.

"Do you ever think of havin one? One for us?" The thought made me all crazy; I hugged him, like I had one billion tiny worms dancin in my veins. He pushed me away, got real serious.

"You not pregnint," he said angry. "You pregnint?"

"No, Smiley, I—"

"You better not get fuckin pregnint or I'm out the fuckin door. You see that door?" he yelled, pointin to it. "I be out it if you get pregnint. I ain't supportin no fuckin baby. Thass that. No way. Be bad enough supportin me an you." He got up, lickin his joint shut. "You got enough H?" he axed before he went into the "bedroom".

"Yeah," I said, feelin like if somethin got taken out. He saw my spression an kinda felt bad, so he came over an kissed me an picked me up like some baby in bed an kissed me again. "Now we don't want no babies, okay?"

"Okay," I said.

An then we fucked.

The necks night I was sittin on the stoop with Diana. It wasn't like I planned it or anythin, it's juss Smiley wasn't home yet an I decided to wait for him outside cause I been in the fuckin apartment all day long, throwin up, mostly. Maybe it was the smoke an the H? I told this girl bout it an she laughed an said, "Uh-ohh," but the bitch vanished before I could get the story out of her.

Anyway, I was gonna hang out for a while, an went down-stairs an I heard cryin, not like screamin or wailin, but soft cryin an sniffin. I looked down the hall way an saw somebody down by the other stairwell that goes to the other side of the buildin, juss the top of a head behind the rail where everybody puts the gar-bage. I walked over, cause I'm a curious bitch, an it was Diana, in a cute blue maternity thing that said BABY an had an arrow pointin to her belly. She heard me an looked up an got all self-concious. We weren't really close or nothin, juss talked once or twice, so I started talkin a whole lot, first bout the smell of the hall way, then garbage. I told her my top ten worst insects list (she cracked up), an then finally I got to axe. "So how come you down here cryin?"

Diana kinda sighed an rearranged her long hair with a toss of her head. She wiped at her face clumsily. "My mother an I had another fight about the baby."

"She still wancha to get rid of it?"

"Yeah. She knows I'm seven months," her voice cracked, "but she don't care. She says she's gonna do whass best for me if she gotta break the law to do it, an she says she'll drag me down if I don't want to. I juss wasn't inna mood for all that shit tonight so I juss stepped out."

"What about your man, where is he?" I tried soundin like a therapist I saw on tv.

"I don't know, Freddie went away. I ain't seen him in six months." She started to cry again an I gave her a hug. She was tremblin a little, juss like Sara's baby when I first picked it up from its crib two weeks ago, when it looked like a tiny red prune. We walked out to the stoop an sat there for a while.

"You think your mother's gonna come down an getchu?" I axed.

"I don't know. She always sends Marissa. She expected me to sit there an hear another sermon bout what I gotta do, but I'm not gonna, I'm not gonna kill my baby," she said firmly, her voice gettin louder, "because it's mines, an Freddie's, an someday he'll come back, an even if he doesn't, so what? The baby is . . . a produck of our love for each other, a part of us, you know? There's a part of me in that baby an if I let her kill it, she'll be killin somethin of mines. . . I feel it, you know? It moves aroun in there. It does bumps an grinds an shit! It's juss waitin to be born. I'm not gonna let her murder my baby!" she yelled, clenching her fists as if she was gonna punch me.

"Don't get so worked up," I said, tryin to calm her down.

"Worked up? Don't get so worked up? You ack like this is somethin trivial, like buyin lechuga o tomate! It's not, you know. It's a baby. An it's mines, dammit, mines!"

"An how you gonna bring it up?" I axed, already gettin too involved, but somethin happens to me when I get yelled at. "If you have it, you gonna stay with your mother?"

"No way. I know a friend who lives near Melrose. She's gettin it ready. In a week I can go live with her."

"So what? How you gonna bring it up? How you gonna feed it? You got money for that, or is your friend also a fuckin bank?"

"She's gonna help me til I get on my feet," she said slowly, like if she was tryin to remember lines from a play.

"Yeah? An how you gonna get on your feet? You leff school?"

"I'm goin back."

"So you still gotta get money. Where's it gonna—"

"Freddie'll help," she said angrily.

"He's halfway to Bermuda by now." I knew that was cruel, but juss who the fuck she think she is, yellin at me like that when I try an help?

"Fuck you!" she suddenly screamed. "You're juss like my mother!"

Thass when Marissa appeared in the doorway, wearing a polka-dot mini-skirt an wooden sandals that clacked real loud.

"Ma says to come up," she said, a finger in her mouth.

"I'm not goin up there, you tell . . ." The words froze in her mouth, cause juss as she turned to tell Marissa off she spotted her mother comin down the hall.

"I'm not comin with you!" Diana screamed, jumpin off the stoop an tryin to run away. This was when her mother put on speed an grabbed her, pullin her to the stoop again.

"Let her go!" I yelled, tryin to untangle them, but I got an elbow in the face real hard from one of em. They both collapsed on the sidealk, Diana screamin "I hate you!" an throwin punches like a demon. Millie, the daughter of the guy who owns the bodega next door started yellin for the cops. Diana's mother was hittin back now, an hard, up on her feet while Diana rolled on the ground from the punches, gettin soaked from a dribblin pump she fell under. Her mother started pullin on her an I thought she'd hurt her or somethin so I lunged, pullin her away.

"Leave her alone!" I screamed.

"Leave her alone?" her mother roared back in my face, her eyes real big. "Leave her alone? With you? She's my daughter, not yours! My baby! An she's not endin up like you!" Her voice was hoarse, her arms flyin aroun like pinwheels, as she gestured wildly at the crowd (which always forms at the first sign of a free show). "Buncha junkies an shits, you gonna save my daughter from me? I'm savin her from dirt like you!" She grabbed Diana again and started draggin her. "Less see you stop me, carajo!" She had completely flipped, her eyes bulgin, her hair a mess, her red blouse all torned up. She kept draggin Diana even though she screamed an swung out at her while scratchin one arm up pretty bad against the sidewalk. Two guys from the bodega came out and pulled her off, because Diana was movin funny, holdin her stomach an movin funny.

"Oh God!" she screamed, louder than anything I ever heard in my life. She wriggled an seemed to fold into a ball, clutchin her stomach. I bent over her, trying to unbend her, me an Millie both tried but we coodent. When she looked up at me her face looked horrible, all cracked inside as if the end had come.

"Oh shit, get a ambulance!" I yelled, at nobody an everybody, while Marissa stood frozen to the spot by the stoop, starin blankly as if watchin tv, absently pullin up on her designer panty hose.

It was a week after that that Sara gave away her baby. She got rid of it somehow, I don't fuckin know how, I juss kept seein her without it so I axed her one day an she juss got this real idiot grin on her face like when she's stoned, an she said, "It's gone," an then she walked away from me with her blarin box, over to her new man by the liquor store with the gleamin pint of brandy. I juss ran home to my H after that, I juss coodent deal with it. I don't know, I don't read much, I don't watch news, don't care bout how many got fried in Nicaragua or Cuba or whatever, but sometimes I get this real bad feelin, an it's not bout politics, cause that guy Matt who turned me on to H was a real militant black mother who was always sayin the system hadda be overthrowed an I think he's still sayin it from his sewer hole somewhere. I don't got a head for that shit, you know? But this feelin I get. I look out my window an see it all crawlin by, see it scribbled on Sara's face, stamped on Diana's torn maternity suit. I remember her mother's words an they all seemed to hit me somewhere. Shit, I even feel it now when I look at myself in the mirror an see the circles under my eyes an the marks on my fucked-up arms: we're in some real serious shit here. It's no place for babies. Not even a place for dogs. I guess I can't pretend I'm alive anymore. Diana's baby was lucky; it died in the incubator. On my seventeenth birthday, I dreamed I was in that incubator, chokin. Smiley woke me up with a cup cake that had a candle on it. He remembered.

Smiley noticed I changed a little, cause I wasn't so happy anymore. I juss wanted to take my H an cruise on my run an not bother. He even got madder cause I din't wanna fuck no more. I din't tell him I was pregnint, not even after four weeks passed.

I saw Diana on a corner, in shorts an Pro Keds, all smiles cause she was high, her eyes lookin like eight balls.

"Lissen," she said. "I was wonderin if like maybe you cood do me a favor an shit? Can you like turn me on to some Horse? I really wanna try it an Sara said you'd turn me on. Whataya say, yeah?"

Somethin inside me popped. I'm not a normally violent person, but like a reflex an shit, I smacked her right in the face, hard. She fell back about three feet against a riot gate that rattled.

"Whachu do that shit for?" she yelled, blood burstin over her teeth from a busted lip. She was breathin heavy like some tough butch. I juss stared at her, then went upstairs to my H.

"Man, you out already?" Smiley said one night in surprise, going through my kit. "I thought you had a week's worth."

Smiley din't know there was a tiny baby inside of me, but I knew it. I also knew there was a part of me in that baby, an a part of him, an zero plus zero equals zero. So I din't say nothin.

I got a abortion.

Notes

"Babies" is a painful story. A young girl—a smart, sensitive young girl—is battered by the hopeless, vicious cycle of poverty. Even though she's tough, I can't be sure she'll survive. And her friends, even more tragic because they don't even question their lives, carry on the cycle because *there is nothing else they can do.* All I could do was nod in silent agreement as this girl chose not to have her baby. I couldn't be happy she'd made that choice; I only felt it was inevitable.

This story made me feel what the people in it feel—hopeless. I could see no way out for them. I could understand why a seventeen-year-old girl would take heroin, and yet slap another girl who wanted to try it. I could understand why someone who had so little would want a child so much, and why she would decide to have an abortion anyway.

I was moved.

And I wasn't the only one. Philip Athans, editor and publisher of *Alternative Fiction & Poetry,* says he "was just floored" after reading "Babies." "This is among the most intense, chilling short stories I've ever read, let alone published."

Athans says the key to this story is its realism. "I can't honestly tell you how real it is—I've never lived in the South Bronx and I've never visited there, by a very conscious choice. So I can't say that this is exactly the way things happen there, the way people talk, and the way people act. But there was something about it that seemed too real to not be true. It rang so true to me that I couldn't resist it. That, to me, is where all of its power lies."

Athans says another reason he was affected by the story was the author's "refusal to go into a sort of cop-out sentimentality, and his refusal to allow all of the many problems he presents to be solved in a nice little package in the end. There really is no solution to any of these people's problems by the end of the story."

Athans is right about where the story comes from. "The reason I wrote it is because of where I live, here in the South Bronx," Abraham Rodriguez says. "Everywhere I looked, I'd see young teenage girls getting prepared for having babies and going on welfare. It's this incredible vicious circle. It just feeds on itself, all these unprepared mothers having kids that are unprepared for anything. It's something that bothers me."

The story came to him easily, he says. He dashed it out in two nights. "It's one of those remarkable things about writing that I'll never understand. You can sit there in front of a typewriter for it seems like years trying to work out these things so they'll come out right and they don't. One night you'll just feel something and write, and it'll come out—you won't even be conscious of it. I can't really take credit for that, it's just something that happens."

Rodriguez says he often writes out of frustration. "Usually when I go running to the typewriter I'm trying to get something out of my system or I feel churned up or I feel some kind of energy, and I have to bash it out. So I grab the old Royal and start punching out this aggression, and whatever comes out comes out. Sometimes it can be a very sweet little story, and other times it's like this."

The aggression comes from what he sees going on around him. "I think the frustration of being surrounded by that and being so help-less—being so helpless about changing the twelve-year-old girls get-ting pregnant and thinking it's cool," he says. "This kind of ignorance drives me crazy. It's a whole atmosphere of ignorance. And it's not just the South Bronx, it's everywhere. Ignorance is wiping out everything."

That may be why the story is so raw, Rodriguez says. "It's a very vicious story. The language is very aggressive. My writing isn't usually as gruff as that, but it's just the way it came out. That's just the girl. That's who she is, and that's how she talks, and that's how she feels."

Rodriguez says the language was a natural choice. "Not be-cause I'm so into making an impression, but because it's something I'm more familiar with than Thomas Hardy language. I love Thomas Hardy, but that language is kind of proper. How many characters talk that way? How many people that I'm writing about talk like that?"

Athans says the language is necessary. "If the people in the story didn't talk the way they did, it would really be reduced to the level of a network TV show and lose every bit of its reality. If you were to remove the 'offending' language, you would really cut a lot of its power."

Even though they thought the language was essential, both Athans and Rodriguez gave some thought to whether it would offend readers. Rodriguez worried that editors would reject the story as too vulgar. It was returned several times, giving him doubts, but eventually his confidence in the story won out. "It took a while, but eventually I just said it's got to go the way it is."

Athans agreed. "I thought that, taking the story as a whole, if the only thing you can find in here to be offended by is the language, you have big problems. There's a lot more in this story that should offend people—people should be offended that this kind of place actually exists in this country at this time."

The most important element of the story, Rodriguez says, is not the language, but the narrator. "I like her a lot, that girl. She doesn't even really have a name—I couldn't give her a name, I thought she was so unusual."

One way she is unusual is her drug habit. "You won't find many Puerto Rican girls around here who are heroin users," Rodriguez says. "You see it fairly rarely. I think I focused on heroin because I wanted to make her unique."

Heroin isn't all that sets her apart. "She's also unique because she thinks about everything so much. That's why at the end she has the abortion," Rodriguez says. "I think when she has the abortion it's sad because she wants to have a baby, but she's realistic."

She also wants to be a writer. "That's something she doesn't talk about in the story—she doesn't talk about anything," he says. "It doesn't seem like she has any future. She doesn't see a way out of her hole. But she did write this story."

Wanting to be a writer fits in with her thoughtfulness, Rodriguez says. "She's analytical enough that she can write about what's happening to her. I figured she wouldn't be the kind of person who would change her language because she's writing—she'd be totally natural."

Trying to let her write naturally presented some difficulties. When he rewrote the story several months after it was published, Rodriguez decided some of the misspellings and odd punctuation seemed affected. He also worried about the incongruity of having her misspell common words but spell bigger words correctly.

He stripped out some of the mistakes, but not all of them. "I decided some of it wouldn't be affected, some of it would be just right. I figured she'd probably look up a word she wanted to use and wasn't sure about, whereas a word like *couldn't* or *shouldn't* she'd be sure about."

The characters of Diana and Marissa "are really more typical of what goes on around here" than the narrator is, Rodriguez says. "Not their mother, though, because that mother gets very upset and tries to drag Diana off. That mother is an exception—a mother who cares that much, that's very rare." In the revised story, the sympathy between the narrator and Diana's mother is stronger, he says.

Writing about Hispanics made Rodriguez uncomfortable at first. "You start getting into this thing, thinking, 'I'm speaking for the masses of oppressed Puerto Ricans.' It gets to your head."

He overcame that by realizing that he wasn't trying to speak for all Puerto Ricans. "I feel like I'm expressing something more personal than Puerto Rican. It's just me I'm writing about, not anyone else. If my stories are sincere, if they're personal, it's because they're real. They're me."

Though he's political, Rodriguez tries to keep that aspect out of his stories. "The trick is when you're venting your spleen not to overstate things and not to sermonize and not to get all political. That kind of stuff is nonsense. You just want to write a good story."

He does that by writing about himself, not just the events that happen around him. For instance, he may write about a man who was shot in the hallway of his apartment building. "The impact it has on me is what creates the story, is what's going to recreate his life someday. Because I feel sorry for that guy, I feel sorry for what's happening here, and I guess I feel sorry to be caught up in it. . . . Sometimes I can see what people are doing more clearly than they can. I can see what people are doing because it hurts me so much."

Rodriguez doesn't always write about life in the South Bronx. "When I first started writing I wanted to get away from the Bronx," he recalls. "The idea wasn't to be here, the idea was to escape it." So he mostly wrote about Europeans.

Now he writes about whatever moves him. "The world is in sad shape and anything that you write is going to reflect your feeling about it," he says. "Not necessarily through Puerto Rican eyes, but through human eyes or human comprehension of pain."

He doesn't worry that he'll lose his motivation even if he leaves the South Bronx. "I could live in Poughkeepsie and feel this, because it's already been stamped inside me. It's not something you forget."

He adds, "As long as I'm frustrated about what happens—and I think that'll be a long time—it'll continue to come out in this way. The frustration can dissipate but I think the feelings are still going to be around."

Do Not Disturb

Get me something to draw. Put it there." She hoists herself slowly and painfully higher on the pillows. She has a pad and pencil in her hand. Her voice is peremptory with hurry.

I look around the room. Nothing seems suitable. What would an artist like to draw for her last picture? Not a hairbrush or a commode or a bedpan wrapped in a towel or an empty glass or a little bottle with a prescription label wrapped around it. I feel bad that there are no flowers. Where have all the flowers gone? She could draw those but I haven't refilled the pots and jars. I think about her voice. How commanding a whisper can be! In the evening when she says, "Read me some poems," I sit in the chair by her bed with an anthology in my lap, turning over the pages. It is as though my mouth is stuffed with an obstinate silence. All good poems are about love or death. How can I read love poems to my dying mother? And death . . . how can I read her those? So I read limericks. She does not laugh. There she lies waiting, full of pain and I, her daughter, *can not read her sad poems*. I choke on them.

So now I look for something for her to draw. On top of the bookcase I find a little driftwood post with two seagulls sitting on it, wings spread. On the base it says 'Provincetown,' a souvenir of someone's trip to New England.

"Is this all right?" I say. "Anything," she answers.

So I put it on the table by her bed. Squinting and tipping her head weakly, she draws a very shaky little picture of the gulls.

"That's *good*," I say. "See, you can still draw."

She looks angrily at the picture and scrunches down in her bed. She pushes the paper onto the floor and closes her squinted eyes.

That squint and tilted head... I slip backwards to a work-place she had long ago full of huge marble pillars. Someone had lent her this big light place with a skylight under a cold north sky. The soles of my bare feet are icy on the marble floor and the light—so cold, so north—makes my stomach contract. It reaches in and turns the backs of my eyes to ice.

I am sitting where I have been put, on top of a post. "Wrap the towel around you if you get cold," says my mother.

I don't put the towel around me. I am little and fat and only cold at the backs of my eyes. "How long...?" I ask. She is making a statue of me with a tail. She wraps my legs in a cloth so that when the statue is finished I have no knees, no calves, no feet. But my scaley tail is supple and lovely. "How will I walk?" I think to myself.

But now in this present, I walk. I walk into the bathroom, rinse her toothbrush, comb the hair out of her hairbrush. Something is making it impossible for me to be the master-of-ceremonies she wants. I can stage manage but I can't make her into a legend. I can't help my mother to be a prima donna of dying. Anyway I know she can do it herself. She knows hundreds of poems by heart. She can say them to herself, surely, without implicating me in this disaster.

She says, "You didn't take away my pills did you?"

"No, they're here. They're safe. I put them on the shelf in the closet."

"Good," she says. "Are they in their bag?"

"Yes," I say, "they are in the bag."

She no longer gets out of bed by herself and I do not offer to get the sleeping pills. I am surprised that she does not ask me to get the bag for her.

Months before she had spread out its contents for me to see. Years ago I had woven the bag and given it to my mother for Christmas. It is still gaily striped with a flap that folds over and fastens on a little bone button. In it I know she keeps a piece of scratch paper with a list on it. It is a list of ways of killing yourself.

Also there are two prayers copied neatly on the backs of stiff invitation cards, a bottle of Nembutol and a bottle of Seconol, and a
sign off the door of a hotel room in Nairobi where she once spent
a few days. The sign says, "Do Not Disturb" in English and on the
other side in Swahili which none of us knows. We have not been
to Africa.

My mother entrusts me with this valuable bag when she
comes home for the purpose of dying. She is afraid nurses or
doctors will dispose of it—all those carefully stored up sleeping
pills. She is even afraid that her husband, my stepfather, might
take it away. She is afraid that they will all keep her alive too long.
Longer than she can draw.

Next morning when I open the drawer in her bedside table
to put away the thermometer, there it is, the little bright striped
bag I made, stuffed to the back of the drawer. My heart does
something funny in my chest, but I close the drawer without saying anything even though she is watching me. I have promised
not to interfere.

We are sitting around her bed trying to persuade her to go.

"But couldn't he come to see me here?" she asks. This doctor who has taken care of her for so many years won't come. He
doesn't make house calls. She knows that. Under the circumstances he is a bastard.

"Mother, PLEASE!" I say.

"I don't want to go to the hospital. Please don't make me."

"We just do the best we can." Her old husband sits by the
window. "We can't do more than that." Helplessly in his hands he
holds the best-seller he has been reading aloud to his wife. She
picked it out. Last night I listened to him reading in his beautiful
educated English voice. He read: ". . . and the archbishop, dressed
only in bathing trunks, put his hand on the girl's breast. Slowly he
moved it down . . ."

"Oh dear me!" said Charles. "It embarrasses me."

"You don't have to read that part if you don't want to. Just
skip," I said, trying to be helpful.

"Oh, no!" my mother's voice small, weak, imperious. "Don't skip. I want to hear that part."

Charles sighed. "... down her silky thigh...."

Now the family is working on her. The doctor may be a bastard but he holds the whip hand. We must comply. Every afternoon she turns to me and says, "This is the hurt-y time. The hurt-y time is just beginning." Her granddaughters, my grown-up children have come to help and they too have watched the pain, the crying she can't help. None of us can stand it any more. So we are begging her to go to the hospital as a sop to the doctor so he'll give her pain killers. But she is afraid she'll be stuck there without her pills, disempowered by the omnipresence of nurses. She is afraid she will lose control of her own death.

Suddenly she sits up very erect in her bed. We all jump. She is infused with strength and flushed with anger. "All right, I'll go," she says. Her younger granddaughter Maggie goes and sits beside her on the bed. "I think you are very brave," she says.

"Thank you for saying that," says my mother and falls back on the pillow. There are tears in her eyes and in Maggie's too.

I wish I had thought of saying that good thing. But I only fumble with the keys to my car which, for some reason, I seem to be holding.

When we get to the hospital I push her wheelchair down the hall. "Ugh!" she says. "Everything in hospitals always smells of tutti frutti. I'll *die* if they give me tutti frutti mouthwash and tutti frutti toothpaste. I hate that smell. Ugh!"

It is Monday morning, I park and enter the hospital through a back door. I have come in the wrong way. Two orderlies in white each wheel two carts along the hall towards a sign which says MORGUE. Each cart has a sheet-covered form on it.

The carts cross my path as I search for the right door. "Sorry," says one of the orderlies, swerving to avoid bumping into me. "We had a bad weekend. This is not a very nice thing to see. I'm sorry." Somehow I don't mind seeing this thing. It doesn't particularly shock me, but I am very impressed with the orderly's concern for my feelings. I walk towards the elevator and as I go I remember hearing that death smells of fruit.

We are all sitting on red leather chairs outside the operating room reading copies of *Sports Illustrated* and not talking. They are doing an exploratory operation. After a very short wait we see the surgeon coming towards us. He pulls his mask down around his neck and peels off his gloves. "She couldn't take the anaesthetic," he says. My heart pounds. "We had to bring her out of it," he says. "We couldn't complete the procedure. Her blood pressure began dropping so fast that we had to bring her out of it. I'll want her in intensive care for the night. She'll be O.K. Here she comes."

My angry mother is being wheeled out of the operating room. I unstick myself from the red leather chair. We all do. We all troop after the cart to the intensive care unit. My mother is furious that they didn't simply let her blood pressure go all the way to the bottom. "What a lot of trouble that would have saved!" she says. "Oh, now!" says the doctor.

But now, since she is still alive, she doesn't want to be in intensive care.

"I'm taking her home," I say, looking fearfully at the tubes, bottles, electric wiring, clamps and pulleys hanging all over the place. I remember the paper signed by my mother and entrusted to me, the guardian of her right to die. I feel its frayed edges in my pocket.

"You can't take her home," says the doctor. "She'll be all right but we need to keep her here overnight."

"O.K. I'll stay with her then," I say. The doctor disappears while I am looking for a chair. The rest of my family are saying goodbye to my mother and leaving. The nurse takes me by the elbow and pushes me through a wide chairless space towards the door. "You can't stay in intensive," she says. "It's against the rules." My eyes fill with tears of frustration. I have seen death with hands strapped down. Can I protect her from all those tubes? I am failing in my trust. I look at my mother who is suddenly sleeping. They haven't stuck any tubes into her yet. Only one harmless little electrode is stuck to her chest so the nurse on duty can see the little green bouncing ball on the screen above her head.

"Look," I say. "Here is this paper signed by her. It says 'Please don't use heroic measures to keep me alive.' See. Right here." I force the paper into the nurse's hands. She tosses it onto a desk we are passing as we move towards the door. "Don't be silly," says the nurse. "She's not going to die tonight."

The nurse is stronger than I am and I allow myself to be pushed out into the hall.

She is home again from the hospital where, after all the tests, they give us no answers, only the pain-killers. Most of what I still think of as her 'vacation' is over. In three days she will go back to the retirement colony. Because that has always been the plan. Charles is looking up plane schedules. He has found out that a stretcher can be put on a plane and I am looking under 'ambulance' in the yellow pages. She is too sick to wait. It is now or never.

We sit around my mother's bed discussing these plans but she makes no comment. I feel dizzy with hypocrisy. She and I know perfectly well that she has come here with the purpose of taking her pills in this little girl room where she slept as a child eighty years ago.

She watches me turn over the pages of the telephone book. "This looks like a good one," I say. "Asclepius Ambulance." It is near the beginning of the ambulance listings. Still in the A's. I carry the book over and show it to Charles. He chuckles and we remember our trip to Greece. My mother was sick but she'd been to Epidaurus before. "I'll wait in the bus," she told us. "Don't forget to look into the snake pit, then sit in the theatre and invite your souls."

Charles goes to the telephone carrying the telephone book. Chicago is a big city and he is old so it takes both hands to hold the book and he loses the place and has to look up 'ambulance' again. My mother watches him without visible emotion.

The sun is setting and she looks out the window to the clouds which hover invitingly at the edge of the western horizon. "Please read me a poem," she says to me. I put on my glasses. The book opens to "Dover Beach." All right for her—I'll read it. I clear my throat.

> ... *The Sea of Faith*
> *Was once too at the full and round earth's shore*
> *Lay like the folds of a bright girdle furled.*
> *But now I only hear*
> *Its melancholy, long, withdrawing roar,*
> *Retreating, to the breath*
> *Of the night-wind, down the vast edges drear*
> *And naked shingles . . .*

She interrupts the poem. "I miss God," she says. "I wish I had never learned about becoming One with the All. It's not a thing I want to do. I loved my personal God better." We never get to the last verse: "Ah, love let us be true to one another! . . ." We do not take each other in our arms and weep. I just straighten the bedclothes, give her toes a perfunctory squeeze under the covers, and go to get her supper, abandoning her to the infinite sunset sky.

She is lying on the sofa in the late afternoon and I am feeding her junket. Little girl food for her who is still my mother. My grandson is sitting beside me. He is six and has a pile of pictures he drew for her this afternoon. He is showing them one by one to his dying great grandmother . . . hoping to please her . . . to make her happy . . . to entertain her while she eats. She tries to look for the sake of the kind and worried little boy. She is trying to be entertained while she eats her supper but it is hard for her to swallow.

She looks out beyond the pictures and the porch through eyes which have gotten very little. I have noticed their littleness in the last few days. It scares me. I don't understand how eyes can shrink but it looks like that. The juice must be draining out of the eyeballs themselves. So it is very hard for her to look at Bertie's pictures. He sighs. He has tried his best but she looks away and out through the double doors. Suddenly a tiny flicker comes to the littleness of her eyes. "Look!" she says, "the dragonflies are hatching!"

We stop watching her and turn. Far off beyond the meadow is the prairie. The late sun slopes onto the tall prairie grass, the giant bluestem with its waving turkey-foot plumes. Above the plumes there is an extraordinary sparkling...acres of little flashes and brightnesses moving. A million sparks fluttering in the sunset light. "They always hatch in the first week of August," says my mother. "Every year you must remember to watch for the sparkle of the baby dragonflies."

Scene:

A dark ancestral room. In a carved four-poster bed in the center death leans against the pillows wearing a clean white night cap. To the right, kneeling or in a drawn up chair, the grieving spouse who holds death's wasted hand. To the left, the long-familiar family doctor (dark suit, white collar) bending at the bedside. As the curtain rises he takes out his watch. The fine gold links of his watch chain keep him elegantly chained to time as he monitors its passage. The capable woman who has been called in to help wears an ample apron, a floppy cap, and carries little glasses about on pretty plates. From time to time she puts them down. She is familiar with all the accoutrements of death. Boiling water is not required (as for a birth) but lots of little drinks of things.

At the foot of the bed descendants will stand in rotation to hear last words. Sometimes they come in pairs to be blessed, sometimes singly to be disinherited. The story varies but the scene is always the same and on the deathbed the central character performs a prescribed role to the last gasp.

This is how my mother really would like it to be. The ancestral room is there in an inappropriately cheerful pale blue version. We've managed that. And some descendants are here, and her sad husband, and me, her daughter. But we have a rented hospital bed, all cranks and springs, and no doctor with a reassuring watch. However, you do what you can.

Tonight is the last night of her vacation. Tomorrow the plane, the ambulance. We called Asclepius. I put her to bed as usual. She brushes her teeth into the bowl I hold. Then Charles reads us all a chapter about the lovesick bishop who has by now become a cardinal. Her things are packed. Her suitcase sits open on a stool by the door waiting for the last things to go in. She has told me what she wants to take. The crumpled drawing of the seagulls lies on top.

There is a glass of orange juice beside her bed—specially requested—and I know she can easily reach the drawer of her bedside table. I say an ordinary goodnight and she does too. We are both fakers.

One by one her great grandsons and her granddaughters come back to speak to her—to say something good. Good bye? Good night? I don't know because I am not there. Her husband goes in last and when he leaves he shuts her door and goes into his room alone.

After a time of silence (my daughters are putting the children to bed) the whistle my mother wears around her neck for calling me, blows from behind the closed door. I go back and sit down on the side of her bed.

"I won't do it if you don't want me to," she says and we begin a new goodnight. My only guideline is that it is *her* death. I hang onto this by my teeth.

"You are a good daughter," she says. Am I that?

"You are a good *mother*," I say.

"No I'm not," she says. What can I give her?

"I love you," I say again. I can't think of my lines. There should be some other honest words. I don't say "Don't." That small not-saying is all I know to do. I am only the property-man. I long ago refused to be in the play. She has to write it herself but I know she would like me to keep her company. She is hoping I will change my mind and stay.

I hug and kiss her one more time. "Goodnight," I say, and I leave her the way one leaves a beloved child alone to choose her own dress for the party. But when I leave the room this time I leave the door a little open so she can see the comforting light in the hall.

I go into Charles's room where I can hear him sobbing.

"I wanted to take her home with me," he says. He holds on to me and I try to rock this other old and unfamiliar child I cannot save. "We do the best we can," he says again when I abandon him to his own struggle with the dark summer night. Do all of us do what we can, I wonder? What can we do? I smell sweat.

As I pass my mother's half open door, I catch a fraction-of-a-second glimpse of her from the hall. She has raised the head of the hospital bed and she has a glass in one hand. She is putting something in her mouth. I walk very fast past her door to Maggie's room where both my daughters are sitting. The great grandsons are asleep now. These mothers are still dressed though and somehow without purpose. On Maggie's bed they are more perched than sitting. They look unsure of what to do. I sit down in a chair and we talk a little, softly, about small things. "Are the boys asleep?" I ask them. "Do you still have the telephone number of the ambulance?" they want to know. For a while we are quiet. My stomach keeps crawling up my throat and I swallow it. They are white, very white, my daughters.

Suddenly from across the hall we hear a loud snore and from one of us is torn a terrible giggle. Is it me giggling? Who is supposed to be the mother around here anyhow?

After a while there is silence all over the house.

"It seems so lonely," says my oldest daughter.

Early in the morning Maggie comes to my room. "It worked," she says. "She's dead."

I go into the blue child's room where she lies curled on her side and grayly still. I pick up the bright-striped bag from the floor and button the bone button on its emptiness. I put it in her suitcase and close the lid, now with the wrong address on its tag. How will I send it?

I can't quite touch my marble mother until I see, on the foot of the bed, the DO NOT DISTURB sign. It is carefully pinned to the blanket, Swahili-side up, to make us laugh.

Notes

In "Do Not Disturb" Alice Ryerson has accomplished one of the most difficult tasks of fiction: she has taken an extremely personal event from her own life and written about it in a way that transcends the particulars of what happened. She has written a story that is about more than her mother's death, or even this character's death, but rather about something universal—loss, grief, and our inability to protect ourselves from them.

Sometimes, Ryerson shows us, you can do only what you can do. This is what her narrator must accept. She cannot stop what is to happen and cannot take part in it. She can't pull off the dramatic death scene in a darkened bedroom her mother would like. She can't keep her from having to go to the hospital one last time. She can't even find the right words to say. But she *can* do nothing:

"I love you," I say again. I can't think of my lines. There should be some other honest words. I don't say "Don't." That small not-saying is all I know to do. I am only the property-man. I long ago refused to be in the play. She has to write it herself but I know she would like me to keep her company. She is hoping I will change my mind and stay.

I hug and kiss her one more time. "Goodnight," I say, and I leave her the way one leaves a beloved child alone to choose her own dress for the party. . . .

Everything in "Do Not Disturb" supports the inevitability of that scene. From the very beginning, the narrator feels incapable of doing what is expected of her. She can't find an object for her mother to draw or a poem for her to hear. She listens as her daughter talks about being brave, and wishes she "had thought of saying that good thing," but instead fumbles with the car keys. At the hospital, she gets lost on the way in, then pushed from the room by a nurse. At every turn she does her best, but it doesn't seem enough.

Ryerson's understanding of what she was writing about and her sense of what belonged in the story—what supported her main idea and what detracted from it—made the story work, her editors say.

"Alice Ryerson comes from having experienced this piece," says Lois Hauselman, one of the editors of *Other Voices*. "Ofttimes a young writer will try to do something that he or she just can't get to; they just haven't lived or experienced life in that way. Ryerson was able to write from a place of understanding."

Dolores Weinberg, executive editor of *Other Voices,* shares that assessment. "It's a very moving story coming from a different place than we usually publish. It's a very good example of the genre of 'death in the family'—you feel something with this story."

Sharon Fiffer, another editor who handled the story (decisions about what to publish are collaborative at *Other Voices*), says understanding is part of a world view that can come at any age, but agrees it's what distinguishes this story. "There's a feeling of seriousness here, and yet it's not the writer taking herself too seriously. It's treating a serious subject with the respect it needs."

Many writers whose understanding of what they're trying to write about comes from having lived it are unable to sort out what from their own experience is valuable, the editors say.

"We get a lot of stories that are filled with a reverence for your own memory—because it's true, because it happened and you want to record every single thing. In this story, there was nothing that didn't fit in, there was nothing she was clinging to because it was true or because it happened. It was fictional truth," Fiffer says.

Ryerson agrees that what's important is the fictional truth. "It is obvious that the inspiration for this story was actually an event in my life—but although much of it happened, it is still fiction because of what is added and what is left out."

Ryerson's background as a poet may have helped her whittle away what was unneeded, her editors say. At the very least, it lent the story a compelling voice. "There was the wonderful juxtaposition of the lyricism and poet's delivery imposed on a terrible, terrible theme," Hauselman says. "That combination was very powerful."

Ryerson's development as a writer went through many twists, complicated by several other commitments. Besides being a wife and mother, she has been a student, school psychologist, and archaeologist. She also founded and ran the Ragdale Foundation, an artists' colony near Chicago.

When she began graduate school, it had to take a back seat to her children. "I already had three young daughters and I had decided that it was okay for me to get an advanced degree as long as they didn't know I was doing it," she recalls. "Then I'd be sure I wasn't taking anything away from them. . . . What a terrible example I set! Sneaking off to do work I loved. For the same dubious reason I didn't take my writing seriously until all four of my children were well launched."

Ryerson had four poems in *Poetry* between 1939 and 1942, but didn't publish again until 1970. Since then her poems have appeared in many small magazines and she has published three books of poetry.

The transformation from poetry to short stories began about three years ago, when she noticed that her poems were turning into stories. She signed up for a fiction writing course at the University of Chicago taught by Molly Ramanujan. "She taught me how to zero in on the subject of a story—how to find it," Ryerson says. "And then she taught me how to communicate the feelings important to the story." She wrote fragments of this story, originally titled "Death Smells of Fruit," in class.

"After the class was over I realized how many pieces of this story I'd already done," Ryerson says. "They fitted unexpectedly together and I spent a month finishing it. It was like having a half-carved stone on my desk and over a few weeks I carved out the rest. Three drafts."

The story was accepted by *Other Voices* right away, and later received an Illinois Arts Council Literary Award. Ryerson has written six more stories since then, one of which has been published in *Whetstone.*

"More even than being published I get encouragement from the very positive reactions of friends and family. I like it that they like my stories—and at last I feel that it's completely okay to take the time to sit at my desk with the door shut and the telephone turned off and work. I don't have to worry about what we're going to eat for dinner or all the undone laundry."

Retirement from children and other careers has helped in several ways, she says. In addition to the support of her husband, Albert, who is also retired and "a generous helper," Ryerson says the ability to change locations frequently has been important. "Each time I go from one place to another I have a great spurt of creative energy. So we do some shuttling—east to west, city to country, and grandchild to grandchild."

She says she hopes to continue her "loosely rooted life" and continue writing. "If I ever have to settle in one place, it will be a room with a big window and the window will have a huge view of both near and far—so I can travel with my eyes at least. There are lots of stories in my head and I hope I can write all of them."

Deborah Joy Corey grew up in New Brunswick, Canada, and now lives in Cohasset, Massachusetts. She has written a collection of stories and a short novel. A short story called "Drivin'" was published in *Ploughshares'* Fiction Discoveries issue.

Jeanmarie Epperly is a unit clerk at HCA-Wesley Medical Center Emergency Department in Wichita, Kansas, and a junior at Wichita State University, where she has been attending classes part-time since 1981. She has written both fiction and poetry and is working on her first novel.

E. S. Goldman worked in advertising in Pittsburgh and New York until his retirement in 1962. He then became a merchant on Cape Cod and retired a second time in 1981. He says he learned to write by writing and reading widely, and has never taken a class or workshop, knows no other fiction writer, and has never kept a journal. "Had I planned earlier in life to become a professional writer, I emphatically would have done all those things and surely saved myself a lot of time and error." He's married to the artist Virginia Goldman and lives in South Orleans, Massachusetts.

Sally Herrin has served as senior poetry reader at *Prairie Schooner* and has taught creative writing at Moorhead State College and the University of Nebraska. She is also a part-time curriculum consultant for the Nebraska State Penitentiary's prerelease program. Since "Little Saigon" appeared, she has had stories accepted by the *New Southern Literary Messenger* and *Long Pond Review*.

Amy Lippman's story, "Private Lies," won *Mademoiselle's* Fiction Writers Contest and was cited in *Best American Short Stories 1987* as one of the year's one hundred most distinguished short stories. She was born in 1963 and grew up in California. She studied fiction, play writing, and poetry at Harvard and was an editor of the *Harvard Advocate*. She lives in New York and Los Angeles, and has made writing her career, working mostly in television.

Regina Marler says that "aside from a first-person account of divorce and drunken suicide" submitted to the *New Yorker* when she was 14, "Sunday" is the first story she tried to have published. Since then her writing has "veered farther toward the 'strange' or fantastic," making it more difficult to sell. She is a graduate student in English Literature at Arizona State University. She is working on prose poems to be used as spoken accompaniment to dance and a small illustrated edition of her story "Gossamer Temple."

David Nicholson is an assistant editor at the Washington Post Book World. He founded and publishes the magazine, *Black Film Review,* and is working on the second draft of a novel called *Seasons,* which he says is about people a lot like Odis and Daisy.

Jim Pitzen served as an infantryman with the First Cavalry in Vietnam's Central Highlands from 1966 to 1967, when he suffered a pressure fracture in his back. He holds a B.A. in English from Bemidji State College and an M.F.A. in creative writing from the University of Montana. "The Village" received the O. Henry Prize in 1987.

Dale Ray Phillips teaches freshman composition at the University of Arkansas. He is currently working on a collection of stories called *What It Costs Travelers,* which will focus on "the things we construct which give us motion" and include "What Men Love For." Phillips is married to the poet Elizabeth Ford and, at the time of this writing, they were expecting their first child.

Richard Plant, a native of Oklahoma, has a bachelor's degree from Oklahoma State University and a master's in writing from Washington University in St. Louis. He teaches writing at Mary Baldwin College in Staunton, Virginia.

Abraham Rodriguez Jr., 27, was born and raised in the South Bronx. He dropped out of high school after less than a year, but later got a high-school equivalency certificate and went on to study at City College of New York. He says he hopes to spend the rest of his life writing and making music with his band, Urgent Fury. *Ashes to Ashes,* his first collection of short stories, will be published soon by Arte Publico Press.

Alice Ryerson is a retired school psychologist and archaeologist, and founder of Ragdale, an artist colony in Illinois. Her poem "Architect" received an Illinois Arts Council Award in 1984. In 1988, "Do Not Disturb" received another Illinois Arts Council Award. Her books of poetry include *Excavation, Matrimonial Picnic,* and *New & Selected Poems.* She has four children and—to date—eight grandchildren.

Other Books of Interest

Annual Market Books

    Artist's Market, edited by Susan Conner $19.95

    Children's Writer's & Illustrator's Market, edited by Connie Eidenier (paper) $14.95

    Novel & Short Story Writer's Market, edited by Laurie Henry (paper) $17.95

    Photographer's Market, edited by Sam Marshall $19.95

    Poet's Market, by Judson Jerome $18.95

    Songwriter's Market, edited by Mark Garvey $18.95

    Writer's Market, edited by Glenda Neff $23.95

General Writing Books

    Annable's Treasury of Literary Teasers, by H.D. Annable (paper) $10.95

    Beginning Writer's Answer Book, edited by Kirk Polking (paper) $12.95

    Beyond Style: Mastering the Finer Points of Writing, by Gary Provost $15.95

    Discovering the Writer Within, by Bruce Ballenger & Barry Lane $16.95

    Getting the Words Right: How to Revise, Edit and Rewrite, by Theodore A. Rees Cheney $15.95

    A Handbook of Problem Words & Phrases, by Morton S. Freeman $16.95

    How to Increase Your Word Power, by the editors of Reader's Digest $19.95

    How to Write a Book Proposal, by Michael Larsen $10.95

    Just Open a Vein, edited by William Brohaugh $15.95

    Knowing Where to Look: The Ultimate Guide to Research, by Lois Horowitz (paper) $15.95

    Make Every Word Count, by Gary Provost (paper) $9.95

    On Being a Writer, edited by Bill Strickland $19.95

    Pinckert's Practical Grammar, by Robert C. Pinckert $14.95

    The Story Behind the Word, by Morton S. Freeman (paper) $9.95

    12 Keys to Writing Books that Sell, by Kathleen Krull (paper) $12.95

    The 29 Most Common Writing Mistakes & How to Avoid Them, by Judy Delton $9.95

    Word Processing Secrets for Writers, by Michael A. Banks & Ansen Dibell (paper) $14.95

    Writer's Block & How to Use It, by Victoria Nelson $14.95

    The Writer's Digest Guide to Manuscript Formats, by Buchman & Groves $16.95

    Writer's Encyclopedia, edited by Kirk Polking (paper) $16.95

Nonfiction Writing

    Basic Magazine Writing, by Barbara Kevles $16.95

    How to Sell Every Magazine Article You Write, by Lisa Collier Cool (paper) $11.95

    The Writer's Digest Handbook of Magazine Article Writing, edited by Jean M. Fredette $15.95

    Writing Creative Nonfiction, by Theodore A. Rees Cheney $15.95

    Writing Nonfiction that Sells, by Samm Sinclair Baker $14.95

Fiction Writing

    The Art & Craft of Novel Writing, by Oakley Hall $16.95

    Best Stories from New Writers, edited by Linda Sanders $16.95

    Characters & Viewpoint, by Orson Scott Card $13.95

    Creating Short Fiction, by Damon Knight (paper) $9.95

    Dare to Be a Great Writer: 329 Keys to Powerful Fiction, by Leonard Bishop $15.95

    Dialogue, by Lewis Turco $12.95

    Fiction is Folks: How to Create Unforgettable Characters, by Robert Newton Peck (paper) $8.95

    Handbook of Short Story Writing: Vol. I, by Dickson and Smythe (paper) $9.95

    Handbook of Short Story Writing: Vol. II, edited by Jean M. Fredette $15.95

    One Great Way to Write Short Stories, by Ben Nyberg $14.95

Plot, by Ansen Dibell $13.95
Revision, by Kit Reed $13.95
Spider Spin Me a Web: Lawrence Block on Writing Fiction, by Lawrence Block $16.95
Storycrafting, by Paul Darcy Boles (paper) $10.95
Writing the Novel: From Plot to Print, by Lawrence Block (paper) $9.95

Special Interest Writing Books

The Children's Picture Book: How to Write It, How to Sell It, by Ellen E.M. Roberts (paper) $16.95
Comedy Writing Secrets, by Melvin Helitzer $18.95
The Complete Book of Scriptwriting, by J. Michael Straczynski (paper) $11.95
The Craft of Lyric Writing, by Sheila Davis $18.95
Editing Your Newsletter, by Mark Beach (paper) $18.50
Families Writing, by Peter Stillman $15.95
Guide to Greeting Card Writing, edited by Larry Sandman (paper) $9.95
How to Write a Play, by Raymond Hull (paper) $12.95
How to Write Action/Adventure Novels, by Michael Newton $13.95
How to Write & Sell A Column, by Raskin & Males $10.95
How to Write and Sell Your Personal Experiences, by Lois Duncan (paper) $10.95
How to Write Mysteries, by Shannon OCork $13.95
How to Write Romances, by Phyllis Taylor Pianka $13.95
How to Write Tales of Horror, Fantasy & Science Fiction, edited by J.N. Williamson $15.95
How to Write the Story of Your Life, by Frank P. Thomas (paper) $11.95
How to Write Western Novels, by Matt Braun $13.95
Mystery Writer's Handbook, by The Mystery Writers of America (paper) $10.95
The Poet's Handbook, by Judson Jerome (paper) $10.95
Successful Lyric Writing (workbook), by Sheila Davis (paper) $16.95
Successful Scriptwriting, by Jurgen Wolff & Kerry Cox $18.95
Travel Writer's Handbook, by Louise Zobel (paper) $11.95
TV Scriptwriter's Handbook, by Alfred Brenner (paper) $10.95
Writing for Children & Teenagers, 3rd Edition, by Lee Wyndham & Arnold Madison (paper) $12.95
Writing Short Stories for Young People, by George Edward Stanley $15.95
Writing the Modern Mystery, by Barbara Norville $15.95
Writing to Inspire, edited by William Gentz (paper) $14.95

The Writing Business

A Beginner's Guide to Getting Published, edited by Kirk Polking $11.95
The Complete Guide to Self-Publishing, by Tom & Marilyn Ross (paper) $16.95
How to Sell & Re-Sell Your Writing, by Duane Newcomb $11.95
How to Write with a Collaborator, by Hal Bennett with Michael Larsen $11.95
Is There a Speech Inside You?, by Don Aslett (paper) $9.95
Literary Agents: How to Get & Work with the Right One for You, by Michael Larsen $9.95
Professional Etiquette for Writers, by William Brohaugh $9.95
Time Management for Writers, by Ted Schwarz $10.95
The Writer's Friendly Legal Guide, edited by Kirk Polking $16.95
A Writer's Guide to Contract Negotiations, by Richard Balkin (paper) $11.95

To order directly from the publisher, include $3.00 postage and handling for 1 book and 50¢ for each additional book. Allow 30 days for delivery.

Writer's Digest Books
1507 Dana Avenue, Cincinnati, Ohio 45207
Credit card orders call TOLL-FREE
1-800-543-4644 (Outside Ohio)
1-800-551-0884 (Ohio only)
Prices subject to change without notice.

Write to this same address for information on *Writer's Digest* magazine, Writer's Digest Book Club, Writer's Digest School, and Writer's Digest Criticism Service.